ALESSANDRO GIORGI

THE
FIGHTING
FA†HERS

CIA-BACKED CATHOLIC MILITIA
IN SOUTH VIETNAM

Schiffer
Military History

4880 Lower Valley Road
Atglen, PA 19310

Other Schiffer books on related subjects
Forever Forward: K-9 Operations in Vietnam, Mike Lemish, 978-0-7643-3345-3
The Advisor: The Phoenix Program in Vietnam, John L. Cook, 978-0-7643-0137-7

Acknowledgments
Thanks to Jack Benefiel for his courtesy and priceless help, to Padre Gheddo (RIP), and to Father Cesare Bullo, as well as to my colleague and friend Van Huyen Truong.

Designed by Jack Chappell
Cover design by Jack Chappell
Type set in Oblique/Times
Translated from the Italian by Ralph Riccio

ISBN: 978-0-7643-6825-7
Printed in India

FSC
www.fsc.org
MIX
Paper from
responsible sources
FSC® C016779

Published by Schiffer Publishing, Ltd.
4880 Lower Valley Road
Atglen, PA 19310
Phone: (610) 593-1777; Fax: (610) 593-2002
Email: Info@schifferbooks.com
Web: www.schifferbooks.com

For our complete selection of fine books on this and related subjects, please visit our website at www.schifferbooks.com. You may also write for a free catalog.

Schiffer Publishing's titles are available at special discounts for bulk purchases for sales promotions or premiums. Special editions, including personalized covers, corporate imprints, and excerpts, can be created in large quantities for special needs. For more information, contact the publisher.

We are always looking for people to write books on new and related subjects. If you have an idea for a book, please contact us at proposals@schifferbooks.com.

CONTENTS

Introduction...4

Chapter 1   Vietnam and Religion...8
Chapter 2   Catholicism in Vietnam 14
Chapter 3   Catholicism in South Vietnam.................................... 20
Chapter 4   Diệm and His Family.. 26
Chapter 5   The Fighting Fathers 46
Chapter 6   Father Augustine Nguyễn Lạc Hóa 54
Chapter 7   Father Bosco 72

Endnotes.. 76
Bibliography 78
Index... 79

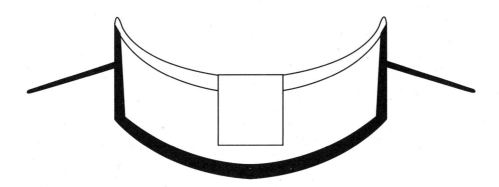

INTRODUCTION

In the research that I carried out in the past to write *Cronaca della Guerra del Vietnam, 1961–1975* ("Chronology of the Vietnam War, 1961–1975"), in examining the memoirs of CIA or special-forces operators, I repeatedly came across references to the so-called Fighting Fathers, Catholic priests who led the armed anti-Communist resistance of their parishioners, arranging for supplies, organizing formations, and at times leading them in operations. The case that piqued my interest the most, and not by accident given my character as a historical researcher, was the most mysterious one of them all. In all the (very few) sources that cited him, he was described as "the most famous": a certain Father Bosco or Brother Bosco. My interest was twofold: on one side, all—and I mean all—the authors who mentioned him limited themselves to saying, "But the most famous of them all was a certain Father Bosco," without adding anything other than, in some cases, the approximate area in which he operated. I asked myself, if he was the most famous, whoever is referencing him must know something other than just his surname; otherwise, on what basis was the historian (if he deserves that title) able to assert that "he was the most famous," other than just having heard it said or, worse but more common, for having "cut and pasted" without digging deeper and verifying the assertion? Every time I was able to track down an author and ask him if he knew why Father Bosco was the most famous, seeing that he (the author) had written as much, the response was always the same: no, he only knew that he had found that information somewhere.

At this point an investigation was called for. The second aspect that raised my curiosity as an Italian was that, given his surname, "Father Bosco," I was led to believe that he was Italian, one of the many Italian missionaries present in the area. Given that Vietnam, in its "American phase," was one of the few wars in which, fortunately, the Italians were not present either officially or unofficially, not even with a field hospital or with advisors undercover, this possible exception, even though "irregular," constituted a very juicy bit of news, if verified. I thus began the usual "pursuit of phantoms."

After having concluded that none of the authors who mentioned him in reality knew anything about him, the logical step was to find, in Italy, priests who had been missionaries in Vietnam during that time period. The first of these, Don Cesare Bullo, who was in South Vietnam from 1962 to 1975, said that he knew nothing, other than that many Catholic refugees from the North had organized into "strategic hamlets," but that in his community of Gò Vấp (a district of Saigon) he dealt with orphans and had no contact with the outside world. However, he provided me with a very useful bit of information: Saint Giovanni Bosco is a very popular saint in the Catholic minority communities throughout Southeast Asia, many children are baptized with the name Bosco, and many priests are called Bosco as a sign of admiration and respect or assume the name of Don Bosco when they are ordained as priests. Thus, the fact that he was called Bosco was not in fact proof that he was Italian; if anything else, it was just the opposite.

The next step, on the basis of a suggestion by Don Bullo, was to contact an authentic authority—Padre Gheddo—who was helpful to me with his book *Catholics and Buddhists in Vietnam*, in which, among other things, there is a very important amount of data regarding the emigration of Catholics from North Vietnam to South Vietnam. In addition, even though he knew nothing directly relating to the question, he confirmed that "Bosco" is a popular name among Catholics of the region. The definitive breakthrough came with contact with Jack Benefiel, the CIA agent who at the time was involved in operations in Father Bosco's area; not only did he confirm that Father Bosco was a "pureblood" Vietnamese, but he provided me with an unpublished and very precious iconography.

By comparison, research concerning Father Augustine Nguyễn Lạc Hóa was much easier, since his public activity was much more visible and politically significant.
Militant Catholic priests in South Vietnam, at the head of their parishioners, transformed them into armed militiamen and trained in guerrilla and counterguerrilla warfare.

Even though seen from a historical perspective through the decades that have passed, a subject of this type still sounds, if not unlikely, certainly surprising. In this book we will look at the history of these units and two of the better-known priests who were involved in those activities.

In order to present a wider picture, the book first examines the various religions found in a country that was and would remain predominantly Buddhist, as well as the role that the Vietnamese president Diệm and his clan played in the historical context we are looking at.

CHAPTER 1

• • • • • • • • • • • • • • •

Vietnam and Religion

• • • • • • • • • • • • • • •

For various reason the Vietnam War was more of a melting pot of a multiplicity of ethnic groups than in other wars. The nations and linguistic, religious, and ethnic minorities involved (more than often against their will) found themselves in the midst of tragic, complicated, contradictory, and extraordinarily interesting historical events.

In addition to a solid Buddhist tradition, onto which were grafted the Confucian and Taoist cultures, were added Christianity, in large part Catholic, some Muslim minorities, and some sects such as the Cao Đài (born in 1926) and the Hòa Hao (in 1939). In the latter case, one must not think of sects with a few thousand followers, grouped in isolated communities; these are sects with seven million followers even today, which are in the majority in certain provinces or districts of the country. Always in the background are obviously the traditional popular Vietnamese religions, in large measure tracing back to the cult of their forefathers.

It is worth noting that all of these Vietnamese sects were in the habit of organizing their own armed militias. The owners of large plantations also had their private militias, as did the bigger opium growers and heroin producers.

HÒA HẢO, CAO ĐÀI, AND OTHER SECTS IN A BUDDHIST COUNTRY[1]

We will concentrate, in our examinations of the Vietnamese religious sects, on the Hòa Hảo and Cao Đài, the most-important ones in that country.

Hòa Hảo

The Hòa Hảo is a cult based on Buddhism, founded in 1939 by Huỳnh Phú Sổ, from the village of Hòa Hảo in the Mekong delta area, in Cochin China (in the south of present-day Vietnam). The Hòa Hảo sect claims to have about two million followers in Vietnam. In some provinces of the delta, more than 90 percent of the population practiced that religion at the time of the facts described.

Huỳnh Phú Sổ (1919–47), considered a prophet by the adherents of this sect, was a sickly young man who suffered from physical ailments and, because of that, was brought by his father to a hermit on Mount Sam at Chau Doc to cure him. In 1939, he returned to his village healed and during a tempest one night decided to reform Buddhism. He was nicknamed "the mad bonze" in Saigon. His troubles began when he began to preach his religion to the peasants. Since his creed was in large part inspired by Vietnamese nationalism, he obviously was politically dangerous during the time of French domination over Indochina. Accordingly, he was committed to the Cho Quan insane asylum for ten months; the result was that in August 1940, thanks to his prophecies, he converted his attending physician to this new nationalist faith. Then he was placed under house arrest at Bac Liêu in May 1941. There he announced a series of prophesies regarding the future of Vietnam.

His Buddhism could not but meet with the favor of the peasants of the delta: no more pagodas, no more lavish and costly ceremonies; the cult is practiced in the home; ceremonies—weddings, funerals—were to be as simple as possible; alcohol and opium were prohibited; and the main preoccupation of each believer was to help those in need. Anti-French, he declared that the "true king" would return to guide the country to freedom and prosperity, which increasingly pushed the Hòa Hảo to support the pretender Nguyễn to the throne: the marquis Cường Để, residing in Japan. All of this drew millions of followers and ended up involving the entire country between the Cambodian border and the "capital" of the delta, Cân Tho. The Japanese, who would later occupy the country, took (not to say "kidnapped") him and installed him in Saigon, hoping to gain members of the sect to their cause. But that did not happen, and the leader of the sect declared that "the Japanese cannot eat the whole chicken" (1945).

In 1942, the French could no longer withstand the growing popular reactions generated by Sổ's oracular pronouncements and political instructions. They exiled him to Laos. By that time, the Japanese had taken over French Indochina but had left the French apparatus in place, intervening only when they saw fit. The Japanese intercepted the transfer of Sổ with the help of some Hòa Hảo followers and brought him back to Saigon. The Kempeitai kept him under protection, and the Japanese authorities rebuffed French protests and demands for extradition by saying that he was held as a "Chinese spy." He avoided accusations of being a Japanese collaborator by predicting their demise, but his contacts with them allowed his supporters to gain weapons. He was considered a mystic.

The Việt Minh, who considered the "crazy bonzo" as a dangerous enlightened man, after having used some of his men against the French, set up an ambush of Huỳnh Phú Sổ on April 16, 1947. He was tried and summarily executed two days later. His corpse was cut into three pieces and buried in different places.[2] The Hòa Hảo were marked by their hatred of the Việt Minh. Huỳnh Phú Sổ was succeeded by truly awful bandits: Trần Văn Soái, an ex-mechanic on the Cân Tho ferry who took the name of Trần Văn Soái (Five Fires) and hid the death of the founder of the sect from the crowds of the faithful. He was an independent bus driver who traveled throughout the region to recruit followers. His third concubine, Lê Thi Ghâm (the Panther), kept the "treasure" collected from taxes from the followers. On May 18, 1947, against all predictions, along with his three hundred armed men, he joined the French, who designated him as a one-star general (this rank, of brigadier general, did not exist in the Vietnamese military tradition, so he bought a second star from a Chinaman). Another leader, Ba Cut ("cut finger," because he had cut off a finger to demonstrate his courage), was a traitor who allied himself five times, each time massacring the French officers who helped him. In the end, after the end of the war in Indochina and the partition of Vietnam into two parts, he was guillotined in public at 5:40 a.m., on July 13, 1965, in Cân Tho by order of Diệm.[3]

Ba Cụt's body was later diced into small pieces, which were then buried separately. Some followers, led by a hard-core deputy named Bảy Đớm, retreated to a small area beside the Cambodian border, where they vowed not to rest until Ba Cụt was avenged. Many of his followers later joined the Việt Cộng—the movement that succeeded the Việt Minh their leader had fought—and took up arms against Diệm.

After having aided the Communists during the Vietnam War, forming a veritable private army, the Hòa Hảo was recognized as one of the country's official religions.

Disciples of Hòa Hảo are obligated to pray to Buddha twice a day, in the morning and in the evening. Alcohol is absolutely forbidden, but during holidays shared with strangers, the faithful can take a small quantity as communion. It is absolutely forbidden to smoke opium. In order to be admitted to the Hòa Hảo, a drug addict has to be detoxified. Gambling is severely prohibited.

Even though Hòa Hảo Buddhism is an officially recognized religion in Vietnam, many members refuse to submit to the Hanoi government, and an undetermined number of religious leaders have been arrested for that reason. In 2005, two Hòa Hảo immolated themselves to protest against religious persecution, and, following a wave of arrests of Hòa Hảo Buddhists, another nine were jailed in May 2007. The Hòa Hảo refuse to believe that their founder died under torture; they are convinced that he is still among the living. Ceremonies that commemorate the birth of the prophet are banned. Since then, the Hòa Hảo has been split into two more or less militant factions.

Cao Đài[4]

Caodaism, or Cao Đài (the official name of the "Church of the Third Revelation")—that is, "High Place," or, according to other versions, "Great Palace"—is a new religious movement founded in 1926 in Tay Ninh (southern Vietnam) by Ngo Van Chieu and other disciples of the Supreme Being. The founders of this cult maintain that they received, during a séance, a revelation from God, who ordered them to create a new syncretic (integrated) religion mixing various elements of Eastern and Western religious doctrines.

The story of that church, monotheist but syncretic, begins in 1919, when Ngo Van Chieu, a functionary in the French colonial administration and a practicing spiritualist, coordinated a series of experiments with several different female mediums. In various séances an entity called "Cao Đài" manifested itself, who presented himself as the highest divinity. Again in a séance, on Christmas night in 1925, it was indicated that the church should be founded and that the aged mandarin Le Van Trung should become its first pope.

The Caodaists believe in one god, who founded the principal religions of the world, such as Zoroastrianism, Judaism, Hinduism, Taoism, Confucianism, Shintoism, Buddhism, Christianity, Islam, and Sikhism.

Caodaist religious practice is founded on prayer, the cult of ancestry, nonviolence (even though, until the recent past, the Cao Đài church had its own private armed militias, which played a role in the various Indochinese civil wars), and vegetarianism, in order to achieve a favorable rebirth through reincarnation or, better yet, to enter paradise and remove oneself from the cycle of life and death.

The "saints" or "spiritual leaders" or epiphanies (manifestations) of the divine are varied in Caodaism. Among them of particular note are the Indian divinity Krishna, the prehistoric mythical Tartar of Indochina as well as the inventor of marital arts, Emperor Huang Vong, Moses, Buddha, Laozi, Confucius, Jesus, Mohammed, Saint Anthony, Joan of Arc, Victor

Hugo (the French writer highly celebrated throughout Asia), Li Bai, and Chinese president Sun Yat-Sen. God is represented as a divine eye.

The cult location par excellence of this religion is Tay Ninh, an architectural masterpiece built during the colonial period. The cathedral vault is held up by eighteen pilasters in the form of dragons that descend wrapped around the pilasters for their entire length and with their heads at the height of the worshipers.

Caodaism has a priestly organization similar to that of the Catholic Church, with a pope, cardinals, bishops, priests, and—in addition, in cases that are more correctly described as unique rather than just rare among faiths that have links to the Bible—mediums. Women are allowed to reach the rank of cardinal.

Adherents believe that the doctrine, symbolism, and organization of Caodaism were directly communicated by God, exactly as construction of the Tay Ninh Holy See was guided by God.

There are seven to eight million followers of Caodaism in Vietnam,[5] to which are added some 30,000 faithful (mainly of Vietnamese origin) in the United States, Europe, and Australia.

Cultural Influence

The militant character of the church—underscored by the presence of private militias and added to an atmosphere of mystery due to the spiritist element—has also inspired some works of fantasy, among them the 1957 science fiction novel *The Ships of Pavlov* by Frederik Pohl and the 1955 novel *The Quiet American* by Graham Greene, from which a celebrated film by the same name was made in 1958, and of which a new version was made in 2002. A large part of that novel narrates the attempts, by various Indochinese factions, to strengthen ties with the Cao Đài church in order to gain support of the militias controlled by the church.

CHAPTER 2

Catholicism in Vietnam

The Catholic Church in Vietnam is part of the worldwide Catholic Church, under the spiritual leadership of bishops in Vietnam who are in communion with the pope in Rome. Vietnam has the fifth-largest Catholic population in Asia, after the Philippines, India, China, and Indonesia. There are about seven million Catholics in Vietnam,[1] representing 7 percent of the total population. There are twenty-seven dioceses (including three archdioceses) with 2,228 parishes and 2,668 priests.[2]

The first Catholic missionaries visited Vietnam from Portugal and Spain in the sixteenth century. The earliest missions did not bring very impressive results. Only after the arrival of Jesuits in the first decades of the seventeenth century did Christianity begin to establish its positions within the local populations in both domains of Đàng Ngoài (Tonkin, the North) and Đàng Trong (Cochinchina, the South). These missionaries were mainly Italians, Portuguese, and Japanese. Two priests, then Italian Jesuit Francesco Buzomi and the Portuguese Diogo de Carvalho, established the first Catholic community in Hội An in 1615.[3] Between 1627 and 1630, Avignonese Alexandre de Rhodes and Portuguese Pero Marques converted more than six thousand people in Tonkin.

In the seventeenth century, Jesuit missionaries including Francisco de Pina, Gaspar do Amaral, Antonio Barbosa, and de Rhodes developed an alphabet for the Vietnamese language, using the Latin script with added diacritic marks. This writing system continues to be used today and is called chữ Quốc ngữ (literally "national language script"). Meanwhile, the traditional chữ Nôm, in which Girolamo Maiorica was an expert, was the main script conveying Catholic faith to Vietnamese until the late nineteenth century.

Since the late seventeenth century, French missionaries of the Foreign Missions Society and Spanish missionaries of the Dominican order were gradually taking on the role of evangelization in Vietnam. Other missionaries active in premodern Vietnam were Franciscans (in Cochinchina), Italian Dominicans and Discalced Augustinians (in eastern Tonkin), and those sent by the Propaganda Fide.

The French missionary priest and bishop of Adraa Pigneau de Behaine played a key role in Vietnamese history toward the end of the eighteenth century. He had come to southern Vietnam to evangelize. In 1777, the Tây Sơn brothers killed the ruling Nguyễn lords. Nguyễn Ánh was the most senior member of the family to have survived, and he fled into the Mekong delta region in the Far South, where he met Pigneau; Pigneau became

Nguyễn Ánh's confidant. Pigneau reportedly hoped that by playing a substantial role in helping Ánh attain victory, he would be in position to gain important concessions for the Catholic Church in Vietnam and help its expansion throughout Southeast Asia. From then on, he became a politician and military strategist.

At one stage during the civil war, the Nguyễn were in trouble, so Pigneau was dispatched to seek French aid. He was able to recruit a band of French volunteers. Pigneau and other missionaries acted as business agents for Nguyễn Ánh, purchasing munitions and other military supplies. Pigneau also served as a military advisor and de facto foreign minister until his death in 1799. Starting in 1794, Pigneau took part in all campaigns. He organized the defense of Diên Khánh when it was besieged by a numerically vastly superior Tây Sơn army in 1794. Upon Pigneau's death, Gia Long's funeral oration described the Frenchman as "the most illustrious foreigner ever to appear at the court of Cochinchina."

By 1802, when Nguyễn Ánh conquered all of Vietnam and declared himself Emperor Gia Long, the Catholic Church in Vietnam had three dioceses, as follows:

- diocese of eastern Tonkin: 140,000 members, 41 Vietnamese priests, 4 missionary priests, and 1 bishop
- diocese of western Tonkin: 120,000 members, 65 Vietnamese priests, 46 missionary priests, and 1 bishop
- diocese of central and southern Cochinchina: 60,000 members, 15 Vietnamese priests, 5 missionary priests, and 1 bishop[4]

Gia Long tolerated the Catholic faith of his French allies and permitted unimpeded missionary activities out of respect to his benefactors. The missionary activities were dominated by the Spanish in Tonkin and the French in the central and southern regions. At the time of his death, there were six European bishops in Vietnam. The population of Christians was estimated at 300,000 in Tonkin and 60,000 in Cochinchina.

The peaceful coexistence of Catholicism alongside the classical Confucian system of Vietnam was not to last. Gia Long himself was Confucian in outlook. Since Crown Prince Nguyễn Phúc Cảnh had already died, it was assumed that Cảnh's son would succeed Gia Long as emperor, but, in 1816, Nguyễn Phúc Đảm, the son of Gia Long's second wife, was appointed instead. Gia Long chose him for his strong character and his deeply conservative aversion to Westerners, whereas Cảnh's lineage had converted to Catholicism and were reluctant to maintain their Confucian traditions such as ancestor worship.

Lê Văn Duyệt, the Vietnamese general who helped Nguyễn Ánh—the future Emperor Gia Long—put down the Tây Sơn rebellion, unify Vietnam, and establish the Nguyễn dynasty, and many of the high-ranking mandarins opposed Gia Long's succession plan. Duyệt and many of his southern associates tended to be favorable to Christianity and supported the installation of Nguyễn Cảnh's descendants on the throne. As a result, Duyệt was held in high regard by the Catholic community. According to the historian Mark McLeod, Duyệt was more concerned with military rather than social needs and was thus more interested in maintaining strong relations with Europeans so that he could acquire weapons from them, rather than worrying about the social implications of westernization. Gia Long was aware that Catholic clergy were opposed to the installation of Minh Mạng because they favored a Catholic monarch (Cảnh's son) who would grant them favors.

Minh Mạng began to place restrictions on Catholicism. He enacted "edicts of interdiction of the Catholic religion" and condemned Christianity as a "heterodox doctrine." He saw the Catholics as a possible source of division, especially since the missionaries were arriving in Vietnam in ever-increasing numbers. Duyệt protected Vietnamese Catholic converts and Westerners from Minh Mạng's policies by disobeying the emperor's orders.

Minh Mạng issued an imperial edict that ordered missionaries to leave their areas and move to the imperial city, ostensibly because the palace needed translators, but in reality in order to stop the Catholics from evangelizing. Whereas the government officials in central and northern Vietnam complied, Duyệt disobeyed the order, and Minh Mạng was forced to bide his time. The emperor began to slowly wind back the military powers of Duyệt and increased this after his death. Minh Mạng ordered the posthumous humiliation of Duyệt, which resulted in the desecration of his tomb, the execution of sixteen relatives, and the arrests of his colleagues. Duyệt's son, Lê Văn Khôi, along with the southerners who had seen their and Duyệt's power curtailed, revolted against Minh Mạng.

Khôi declared himself in favor of the restoration of the line of Prince Cảnh. This choice was designed to obtain the support of Catholic missionaries and Vietnamese Catholics, who had been supporting the Catholic line of Prince Cảnh. Lê Văn Khôi further promised to protect Catholicism. In 1833, the rebels took over southern Vietnam, with Catholics playing a large role. Two thousand Vietnamese Catholic troops fought under the command of Father Nguyễn Văn Tâm.

The rebellion was suppressed after three years of fighting. Father Joseph Marchand, a French missionary of the Paris Foreign Missions Society, was captured in the siege and had been supporting Khôi, and he asked for the help of the Siamese army through communications to his counterpart in Siam, Father Jean-Louis Taberd. This showed the strong Catholic involvement in the revolt, and Father Marchand was executed.

The failure of the revolt had a disastrous effect on the Christians of Vietnam. New restrictions against Christians followed, and demands were made to find and execute remaining missionaries. Anti-Catholic edicts to this effect were issued by Minh Mạng in 1836 and 1838. In 1836–37, six missionaries were executed: Ignacio Delgado, Dominico Henares, José Fernández, François Jaccard, Jean-Charles Cornay, and Bishop Pierre Borie.[5] The villages of Christians were destroyed and their possessions confiscated. Families were broken apart. Christians were branded on the forehead with *ta dao*, "false religion." It is believed that between 130,000 and 300,000 Christians died in the various persecutions. The 117 proclaimed saints represent the many unknown martyrs.

CHAPTER 3

. . . .

Catholicism in South Vietnam

. . . .

From 1954 to 1975, Vietnam was split into North and South Vietnam. During a three-hundred-day period when the border between the two sides was temporarily open, many North Vietnamese Catholics fled southward out of fear that they would be persecuted by the Việt Minh.

In a country where Buddhists were the majority, President Ngô Đình Diệm's policies generated claims of religious bias even though he sponsored and supported many Buddhist organizations, and Buddhism flourished under his regime.

The white-and-gold "Vatican flag" was regularly flown at all major public events in South Vietnam. The newly constructed Huế and Đà Lạt universities were placed under Catholic authority.

In May 1963 in the central city of Huế, where Diệm's elder brother Pierre Martin Ngô Đình Thục was archbishop, Buddhists were prohibited from displaying the Buddhist flag during the sacred Buddhist Vesak celebrations. A few days earlier, Catholics were encouraged to fly religious—that is, papal—flags at the celebration in honor of Thục's anniversary as bishop. Both actions technically violated a rarely enforced law that prohibited the flying of any flag other than the national one, but only the Buddhist flags were prohibited in practice. This prompted a protest against the government, which was violently suppressed by Diệm's forces, resulting in the killing of nine civilians. This in turn led to a mass campaign against Diệm's government during what became known as the Buddhist crisis. Diệm was later deposed and assassinated on November 2, 1963. Recent scholarship reveals significant understandings about Diệm's own independent agenda and political philosophy. The Personalist Revolution under his regime promoted religious freedom and diversity to oppose communism's atheism. However, this policy itself ultimately enabled Buddhist activists to threaten the state that supported their religious liberty.

CURRENT TIME

The first Vietnamese bishop, Jean-Baptiste Nguyễn Bá Tòng, was consecrated in 1933 at St. Peter's Basilica by Pope Pius XI. The Catholic Bishops' Conference of Vietnam was founded in 1980. In 1976, the Holy See made Archbishop Joseph-Marie Trịnh Như Khuê the first Vietnamese cardinal. Joseph-Marie Cardinal Trịnh Văn Căn (in 1979), and Paul-Joseph Cardinal Phạm Đình Tụng (in 1994) were his successors. The well-known Vietnamese cardinal Francis Xavier Nguyễn Văn Thuận, who was imprisoned by the Communist regime from 1975 to 1988 and spent nine years in solitary confinement, was nominated as secretary of the Pontifical Council for Justice and Peace and made its president in 1998. On February 21, 2001, he was elevated to the College of Cardinals by Pope John Paul II. Vietnamese Catholics who died for their faith from 1533 to the present day were canonized in 1988 by John Paul II as "Vietnamese Martyrs." On March 26, 1997, the beatification process for the Redemptorist brother Marcel Nguyễn Tân Văn was opened by Cardinal Nguyễn Văn Thuận in the diocese of Belley-Ars, France.

Vietnam remains the only Asian Communist country to have an unofficial representative of the Vatican in the country and has held official to unofficial meetings with the Vatican's representatives both in Vietnam and the Holy See—such representatives aren't appointed to serve in China, North Korea, or Laos—due to long and historical relations between Vietnam and the Catholic Church. This has improved in a more favorable manner since the Holy See announced that they would have a permanent representative in Vietnam beginning in 2018.

Restrictions on Catholic life in Vietnam and the government's desired involvement in the nomination of bishops remain obstacles in bilateral dialogues. In March 2007, Thaddeus Nguyễn Văn Lý (b. 1946), a dissident Catholic priest, was sentenced by Vietnamese court in Huế to eight years in prison on grounds of "antigovernment activities." Nguyễn, who had already spent fourteen of the past twenty-four years in prison, was accused of being a founder of a prodemocracy movement, Bloc 8406, and a member of the Progression Party of Vietnam.

On September 16, 2007, the fifth anniversary of Cardinal Nguyễn Văn Thuận's death, the Catholic Church began the beatification process for him. Benedict XVI expressed "profound joy" at the news of the official opening of the beatification cause. Vietnamese Catholics reacted positively to the news of the beatification. In December 2007, thousands of Vietnamese Catholics marched in procession to the former Apostolic Nunciature in Hanoi and prayed there twice, aiming to return the property to the local church. The building was located at a historic Buddhist site until it was confiscated by the French colonists and given to Catholics, before the Communist North Vietnamese government confiscated it from the Catholic Church in 1959. This was the first mass civil action by Vietnamese Catholics since the 1970s. Later the protests were supported by Catholics in Hồ Chí

Minh City and Hà Đông, who made the same demands for their respective territories. In February 2008, the governments promised to return the building to the Catholic Church. However, in September 2008 the authorities changed their position and decided to demolish the building to create a public park.

There are twenty-seven dioceses, including three archdioceses: Hanoi, Huế, and Hồ Chí Minh City (former Saigon). In what follows, we shall see how the Catholic religion was intertwined with politico-military events in Vietnam.

Especially after the French defeat at Điện Biên Phủ in May 1954, the Vietnamese Catholic minority (in a country that had a traditionally Buddhist majority) was among the most determined to fight against the Communist faction, which, after having taken power in the North, sought to unify the country under its leadership, conquering the South as well.

After the Geneva Accords of 1954, and the subsequent division (theoretically only temporary) between the two Vietnams, a great number of civilians resident in the North immigrated to the South, and the majority were Catholics. Almost one million Catholics fled from North to South Vietnam in the 1950s after the decisive takeover by the Việt Minh: by 1955, the number was already 676,384, out of 860,206 civilians fleeing to the South, a total that was to increase significantly over the next few years, without counting the over 124,000 military refugees of the French colonial army, leaving only 833,468 Catholics in the North (statistics from 1964), and they were more than inclined, partly because of the favorable position obtained thanks to President Diệm, their coreligionist, to oppose the establishment of the Communist regime in the South also.

Of the 90,000 Việt Minh sympathizers residing in the South who, vice versa, immigrated to the North, around five thousand to ten thousand were left in the South to act as a "fifth column," and others constituted a base from which the early infiltrations to the South were drawn.

With the progressive infiltration of Communist forces in the South, concomitant with political leadership of South Vietnam under the dictator Diệm, who was a representative of the Catholic minority (which was privileged under French rule), between the end of the 1950s and the beginning of the sixties, an organization emerged, in part spontaneous and in part organized by the CIA (under the constant and zealous control of the Saigon government) of armed Catholic resistance in the villages and neutral areas.

The initial American approach (until the 1950s) was that of "Stay Behind," exactly as in Europe; that is, the organization of a clandestine network able to transform itself into active resistance in case of Communist invasion. Among the principal American protagonists of this operation were Ed Lansdale and William Colby.

Edward Lansdale (1908–87), a veteran of the OSS and of military intelligence in the Second World War, then transitioning to the CIA, but always with a parallel cover career in the US Air Force, had played a role in the counterinsurrection fighting in the Philippines in the postwar period against the Hukbalahap Communist movement. In 1953, he was part of the American mission in Indochina that would later become the American military support structure in South Vietnam. At first, Lansdale was a counterguerrilla special-operations advisor with the French forces fighting the Việt Minh, in light of his similar experience in the Philippines. From 1954 to 1957, he led the Saigon Military Mission (SMM) and during that period was actively engaged in training the newly constituted South Vietnamese national army, also organizing the Cao Đài militias commanded by Trình Minh Thế (who was an officer trained in a Japanese Kempei Tai military police officer school, when occupying Japanese forces had begun to see the Cao Đài militias as paramilitary forces; Trình Minh Thế would be assassinated in 1955 under circumstances that were never made clear), with a proposal to support the Vietnamese national army, activating a propaganda campaign to encourage Vietnamese Catholics in the North to immigrate to the South, in the context of Operation Passage to Freedom, and spreading the word that North Vietnamese agents were attacking South Vietnam (which actually happened, but only later).

From 1957 to 1963, Lansdale returned to the Department of Defense in Washington, DC, working as deputy assistant secretary for special operations (as well as a member of the staff of the Presidential Committee for Military Assistance), where he was mainly involved in efforts to over-throw or directly eliminate Fidel Castro from Cuba (Operation Mongoose). This did not, however, prevent him from still being involved with Vietnam.

In 1961, in fact, Lansdale helped publish the story of Father Nguyễn Lạc Hóa, the Fighting Father, who had organized an assault militia called the Sea Swallows from his village of Chinese Catholic anti-Communist exiles and refugees.

The other American director of the operation was William Colby, the future CIA director, who since 1959 had been serving in the CIA station in Saigon, later to become its chief and remaining there until 1962, with the mission of developing South Vietnamese counterguerrilla capabilities in rural areas and to support the Diệm regime, developing a relationship with Diệm himself and with his family, especially with his brother, Ngô Đình Nhu. Before serving in Vietnam, Colby had spent his happiest years at the CIA station in Rome, and before that he had set up the "Stay Behind" network in Scandinavia, especially in Sweden. In 1962, he returned to Washington to become vice chief and then chief of the Far East division of the CIA. Colby maintained that "the key to [winning] the war in South Vietnam was the war in the villages." We might add, as a matter of interest, that Colby was himself a fervent Catholic (his two daughters received their first Holy Communion in Saint Peter's Basilica), so much so that his nickname in the CIA was "the warrior priest."

However, in the field in Vietnam, the person responsible and the co-ordinator of these CIA activities between 1960 and 1964 was Col. Gilbert Layton (1911–96; a former cavalry officer and a veteran of Bastogne, who joined the CIA in 1950), who controlled the agents spread throughout the territory and who, with respect to the Fighting Fathers, acted in the same role that American military advisors played alongside the regular South Vietnamese army.

Given the heavy and incessant North Vietnamese activity, Vietnamese villages progressed from self-defense organization to offensive operations. A "Combat Youth" organization was constituted among Catholics of various ethnicities, which at the time of its greatest expansion, between 1965 and 1966, numbered 39,000 men.

There was the "Catholic Youth," enlisted among the Vietnamese, while the so-called Sea Swallows were enlisted among Vietnamese Catholics of Chinese ethnicity. The promoters and organizers of these armed formations were their pastors, the Fighting Fathers.

From the author's *Cronaca della Guerra del Vietnam, 1961–1975*: "December 31, 1962. There are now over 4,500 members of the "Combat Youth," Catholic volunteers of various ethnic backgrounds, armed and trained by the CIA to defend against the Việt Cộng in the most disputed areas of South Vietnam under the guidance of the 'Fighting Fathers.'"

CHAPTER 4

Diệm and His Family

Ngô Đình Diệm, the future president and dictator of South Vietnam, was born in 1901 in Quảng Bình, a province in central Vietnam. His family originated in Phú Cam Village, a Catholic village adjacent to Huế. His ancestors had been among Vietnam's earliest Catholic converts in the seventeenth century. Diệm was given a saint's name at birth, Gioan Baotixita (a Vietnamized form of Jean-Baptiste), following the custom of the Catholic Church. The Ngô-Đình family suffered under the anti-Catholic persecutions of Emperors Minh Mạng and Tự Đức. In 1880, while Diệm's father, Ngô Đình Khả (1850–1925), was studying in British Malaya, an anti-Catholic riot led by Buddhist monks almost wiped out the Ngô-Đình clan. Over one hundred members of the Ngô clan were "burned alive in a church, including Khả's parents, brothers, and sisters."

Ngô Đình Khả was educated in a Catholic school in British Malaya, where he learned English and studied a European-style curriculum. He was a devout Catholic and scrapped plans to become a Roman Catholic priest in the late 1870s. He worked for the commander of the French armed forces as an interpreter and took part in campaigns against anticolonial rebels in the mountains of Tonkin during 1880. He rose to become a high-ranking mandarin, the first headmaster of the National Academy in Huế (founded in 1896), and a counselor to Emperor Thành Thái under the French colonial regime. He was appointed minister of the rites and chamberlain and keeper of the eunuchs. Despite his collaboration with the French colonizers, Khả was "motivated less by Francophilia than by certain reformist ambitions." Like Phan Châu Trinh, Khả believed that independence from France could be achieved only after changes in Vietnamese politics, society, and culture had occurred. In 1907, after the ouster of Emperor Thành Thái, Khả resigned his appointments, withdrew from the imperial court, and became a farmer in the countryside.

After the tragedy that had befallen his family, Khả decided to abandon study for the priesthood and married. After his first wife died childless, Khả remarried and had twelve children with his second wife, Phạm Thị Thân (in a period of twenty-three years), of whom nine survived infancy— six sons and three daughters. These were Ngô Đình Khôi, Ngô Đình Thị Giao, Ngô Đình Thục, Ngô Đình Diệm, Ngô Đình Thị Hiệp, Ngô Đình Thị Hoàng, Ngô Đình Nhu, Ngô Đình Cẩn, and Ngô Đình Luyện. As a devout Roman Catholic, Khả took his entire family to daily morning mass and encouraged his sons to study for the priesthood. Having learned both Latin and classical Chinese, Khả strove to make sure his children were well educated both in Christian scriptures and Confucian classics. During his childhood, Diệm labored in the family's rice fields while studying at a French Catholic primary school (Pellerin School) in Huế, and he later entered a private school started by his father, where he studied French, Latin, and classical Chinese. At the age of fifteen he briefly followed his elder brother, Ngô Đình Thục, who would become Vietnam's highest-ranking Catholic bishop, into seminary. Diệm swore himself to celibacy to prove his devotion to his faith but found monastic life too rigorous and decided not to pursue a clerical career. According to military historian Mark Moyar (*Triumph Forsaken: The Vietnam War, 1954–1965*), Diệm's personality was too independent to adhere to the disciplines of the church, while British historian Edward Jarvis (author of Thuc's biography, *Sede Vacante: The Life and Legacy of Archbishop Thuc*) recalls Ngô Đình Thục's ironic observation that the church was "too worldly" for Diệm. Diệm also inherited his father's antagonism toward the French colonialists who occupied his country.

At the end of his secondary schooling at Lycée Quốc học, the French lycée in Huế, Diệm's outstanding examination results elicited the offer of a scholarship to study in Paris. He declined and, in 1918, enrolled at the prestigious School of Public Administration and Law in Hanoi, a French school that prepared young Vietnamese to serve in the colonial administration. It was there that he had the only romantic relationship of his life, when he fell in love with one of his teachers' daughters. After she chose to persist with her religious vocation and entered a convent, he remained celibate for the rest of his life. Diệm's family background and education, especially Catholicism and Confucianism, had influences on his life and career and on his thinking on politics, society, and history. According to American historian Edward Miller (in his *Misalliance: Ngo Dinh Diệm, the United States, and the Fate of South Vietnam*), Diệm "displayed Christian piety in everything from his devotional practices to his habit of inserting references to the Bible into his speeches"; he also enjoyed showing off his knowledge of classical Chinese texts.

He considered following his brother Ngô Đình Thục (later Catholic archbishop of Hue, and the highest Catholic authority in South Vietnam) into the priesthood, but eventually chose to pursue a civil-service career.

During his career as a mandarin, Diệm was known for his workaholism and incorruptibility, and as a Catholic leader and nationalist. Catholic nationalism in Vietnam during the 1920s and 1930s facilitated

Diệm's ascent in his bureaucratic career. Diệm's rise was also facilitated through Ngô Đình Khôi's marriage to the daughter of Nguyễn Hữu Bài (1863–1935), the Catholic head of the Council of Ministers at the Huế court, and he also supported the indigenization of the Vietnamese Church and more administrative powers to the monarchy. Nguyễn Hữu Bài was highly regarded among the French administration, and Diệm's religious and family ties impressed him and he became Diệm's patron. The French were impressed by his work ethic but were irritated by his frequent calls to grant more autonomy to Vietnam. Diệm replied that he contemplated resigning but encouragement from the populace convinced him to persist. In 1925, he first encountered Communists distributing propaganda while riding horseback through the region near Quảng Trị. Revolted by calls for violent socialist revolution contained in the propaganda leaflets, Diệm involved himself in anti-Communist activities for the first time, printing his pamphlets.

He progressed rapidly in the court of Emperor Bảo Đại. In 1929, he was promoted to the governorship of Bình Thuận Province and was known for his work ethic. In 1930 and 1931, he helped the French suppress the first peasant revolts organized by the Communists. According to Fall, Diệm put the revolution down because he thought it could not sweep out the French administration but might threaten the leadership of the mandarins. In 1933, with the ascension of Bảo Đại to the throne, Diệm accepted Bảo Đại's invitation to be his interior minister following lobbying by Nguyễn Hữu Bài. Soon after his appointment, Diệm headed a commission to advise on potential administration reforms. After calling for the French administration to introduce a Vietnamese legislature and many other political reforms, he resigned after three months in office when his proposals were rejected. Diệm denounced Emperor Bảo Đại as "nothing but an instrument in the hands of the French administration" and renounced his decorations and titles from Bảo Đại. The French administration then threatened him with arrest and exile.

For the next decade, Diệm lived as a private citizen with his family in Huế, although he was kept under surveillance. He spent his time reading, meditating, attending church, gardening, hunting, and in amateur photography. Diệm also conducted extensive nationalist activities during those twenty-one years, engaging in meetings and correspondence with various leading Vietnamese revolutionaries, such as his friend, Phan Bội Châu, a Vietnamese anticolonial activist whom Diệm respected for his knowledge of Confucianism, and arguing that Confucianism's teachings could be applied to a modern Vietnam. With the start of the World War II in the Pacific, seeing an opportunity for Vietnam to challenge French colonization, he attempted to persuade the Japanese forces to declare independence for Vietnam in 1942 but was ignored. Diệm also tried to establish relationships with Japanese diplomats, army officers, and intelligence operatives who supported Vietnam's independence. In 1943, Diệm's Japanese friends helped him contact Prince Cường Để, an anticolonial activist who was in exile in Japan. After contacting Cường Để, Diệm formed a secret political party, the Association for the Restoration of Great Vietnam (Việt Nam Đại Việt Phục Hưng Hội), which was dominated by his Catholic allies in Huế. When its existence was discovered in the summer of 1944, the French declared Diệm to be subversive and ordered his arrest. He flew to Saigon under Japanese military protection, staying there until the end of World War II.

In 1945, after the coup against French colonial rule, the Japanese offered Diệm the post of prime minister in the empire of Vietnam under Bảo Đại, which they organized upon leaving the country. He initially declined but then reconsidered his decision and attempted to reverse the refusal. However, Bảo Đại had already given the post to Trần Trọng Kim. In September 1945, after the Japanese withdrawal, Hồ Chí Minh proclaimed the Democratic Republic of Vietnam, and in the northern half of Vietnam his Việt Minh began fighting the French administration. Diệm attempted to travel to Huế to dissuade Bảo Đại from joining Hồ but was arrested by the Việt Minh along the way and exiled to a highland village near the border. He might have died of malaria, dysentery, and influenza had the local tribesmen not nursed him back to health. Six months later, he was taken to meet Hồ, who recognized Diệm's virtues and, wanting to extend the support for his new government, asked Diệm to be a minister of the interior. Diệm refused to join the Việt Minh, assailing Hồ for the murder of his brother Ngô Đình Khôi by Việt Minh cadres.

In 1945, Diệm was captured by the forces of the Communist leader Ho Chi Minh, who invited Diệm to join Ho's independent government in the newly declared Democratic Republic of Vietnam (North Vietnam), hoping that Diệm's presence would win Catholic support. Diệm rejected the proposal, however, and went into self-imposed exile, living abroad for most of the next decade. Recognizing his political status, Diệm decided to leave Vietnam in 1950.

In 1951, he secured an audience with Secretary of State Dean Acheson. During the next three years, he lived at the Spellman house at Maryknoll Junior Seminary in Lakewood Township, Ocean County, New Jersey (now closed), and occasionally at the Maryknoll Seminary in Ossining, Westchester County, New York. Then from 1953 to 1954, Diệm attended the Saint Andrew's Abbey, in Bruges, Belgium. During this time, Diệm met Cardinal Francis Joseph Spellman and the then senator John F. Kennedy. (*Note*: There were six or so buildings on the campus at the Maryknoll Seminary in Lakewood, New Jersey, each of which had a name. The name of the building that housed all the faculty priests, plus Diệm, was named the Spellman house.)

Memories from Some of Diệm's Fellow Students at Maryknoll

Source: http://www.voith-usa.com/SemPix/ArmedServices/ Diệm_At_Maryknoll/index.html. Accessed in June 2022.

Ngo Dinh Diệm, the future president of South Vietnam, was exiled in the late 1940s, and was later invited to live in exile at the Maryknoll Seminary in Lakewood, New Jersey, by Maryknoll Fr. Thomas O'Melia. Since Lakewood was not too distant from Washington, DC, it allowed Diệm the opportunity to conduct whatever he might need to right things with his home country. Diệm only spoke French, besides Vietnamese, so those of us in the French class took turns being his guestmaster, cleaning his room, serve his meals, etc. I always enjoyed talking with him, and taking walks with him around the property. He was such a gentleman, but very quiet and unassuming. I believe he started living at Lakewood seminary around 1951. Our class was stationed there in 1950–51, before we were returned to GE [general education] for our third and fourth years before going to Novitiate.

Diệm attended daily Mass while at Lakewood seminary. Whenever we would walk together around the property, he always had his camera with him and loved to take pictures of the scenery. On family visitation days, he kept busy taking pictures of the seminarians with their family.

Those who had up[-]close[-]and[-]personal contacts with Diệm at Maryknoll were part of history. Or maybe it was just another room to clean or practice your French. He finally left MM [short for Maryknoll] to get to Washington, DC, in his attempt to make friends in high places to advance his personal/patriotic goals.

The late Brendan Branley was at the 'Knoll when Diệm was hanging out there. Branley said as soon as he was asked to perform manual labor to earn his keep, that was the end of him!

Those of us who knew him were saddened to learn of his and his brother Bishop's assassination [Bishop Thuc was not murdered; it was his other brother, Nhu, chief of the secret police, who was murdered. A third brother, Can, was executed a few months later].

In Rome, Diệm had obtained an audience with Pope Pius XII at the Vatican before undertaking further lobbying across Europe. He also met with French and Vietnamese officials in Paris and sent a message indicating that he was willing to be the prime minister of the state of Vietnam to Bảo Đại. But Bảo Đại then refused to meet him. Diệm returned to the United States to continue building support among Americans. Nonetheless, to Americans, the fact that Diệm was an anti-Communist was not enough to distinguish him from Bảo Đại and other state of Vietnam leaders. Some American officials worried that his devout Catholicism could hinder his ability to mobilize support in a predominantly non-Catholic country. Diệm recognized that concern and broadened his lobbying efforts to include a development focus in addition to anticommunism and religious factors. Diệm was motivated by the knowledge that the US was enthusiastic in applying their technology and knowledge to modernize postcolonial countries. With the help of Wesley Fishel,[1] then at Michigan State University (MSU), Diệm was appointed as a consultant to MSU's Government

Research Bureau. MSU was administering government-sponsored assistance programs for Cold War allies, and Diệm helped Fishel lay the foundation for a program later implemented in South Vietnam, the Michigan State University Vietnam Advisory Group.

In May 1954, the French had surrendered at Diện Biên Phủ, while the Geneva Conference had already begun in April 1954. On June 16, 1954, Diệm met with Bảo Đại in France and agreed to be the prime minister if Bảo Đại would give him military and civilian control. On June 25, 1954, Diệm returned after several years from exile, arriving at Tan Son Nhut airport in Saigon. On July 7, 1954, Diệm established his new government with a cabinet of eighteen people and was appointed prime minister by Bảo Đại, the head of the Western-backed state of Vietnam. The Geneva Accords were signed soon after he took office, formally partitioning Vietnam along the seventeenth parallel. Diệm soon consolidated power in South Vietnam, aided by his brother Ngô Đình Nhu. After a rigged referendum in October 1955, he proclaimed the creation of the Republic of Vietnam, with himself as president, ousting the emperor. His government was supported by other anti-Communist countries, most notably the United States. Diệm pursued a series of nation-building schemes, emphasizing industrial and rural development. From 1957 onward, he was faced with a Communist insurgency backed by North Vietnam, eventually formally organized under the banner of the Việt Cộng.

The Americans' assessments of Diệm were varied. Some were unimpressed with him, but some admired him. Diệm gained favor with some high-ranking officials, such as Supreme Court justice William O. Douglas, Roman Catholic cardinal Francis Spellman, Representative Mike Mansfield of Montana, and Representative John F. Kennedy of Massachusetts, along with numerous journalists, academics, and the former director of the Office of Strategic Services, William J. Donovan. Although he did not succeed in winning official support from the US, his personal interactions with American political leaders promised the prospect of gaining more support in the future. Mansfield remembered that after the luncheon with Diệm held on May 8, 1953, he felt that "if anyone could hold South Vietnam, it was somebody like Ngô Đình Diệm."

During Diệm's exile, his brothers Nhu, Cẩn, and Luyện played important roles in helping him build international and internal networks and support in different ways for his return to Vietnam. In the early 1950s, Nhu established the Cần Lao Party, which played a key role in helping Diệm attain and consolidate his power.

COUNTERINSURGENCY

During his presidency, Diệm strongly focused on his central concern: internal security to protect his regime as well as maintain order and social change: staunch antisubversion and antirebellion policies. After the Bình Xuyên, an organized crime syndicate militia (with important connections with the police), was defeated and the Hòa Hảo and Cao Đài were subdued, Diệm concentrated on his most serious threat: the Communists. Diệm's main measures for internal security were threats, punishment, and intimidation. His regime countered North Vietnamese and Communist subversion (including the assassination of over 450 South Vietnamese officials in 1956) by detaining tens of thousands of suspected Communists in "political re-education centers." The North Vietnamese government claimed that over 65,000 individuals were imprisoned and 2,148 killed in the process by November 1957. According to Gabriel Kolko, by the end of 1958, 40,000 political prisoners had been jailed.

By the end of 1959, Diệm was able to entirely control each family, and the Communists had to suffer their "darkest period" in their history. Membership declined by two-thirds, and they had almost no power in the countryside of South Vietnam. Diệm's repression extended beyond Communists to anti-Communist dissidents and anticorruption whistleblowers. In 1956, after the "Anti-Communist Denunciation Campaign," Diệm issued ordinance no. 6, which placed anyone who was considered a threat to the state and public order in jail or house arrest.

Nevertheless, Diệm's hard policies led to fear and resentment in many quarters in South Vietnam and negatively affected his relations with the US in terms of counterinsurgent methods. On February 22, 1957, when Diệm delivered a speech at an agricultural fair in Ban Mê Thuột (or Buôn Mê Thuột, the capital city of Đắk Lắk province), a Communist named Hà Minh Trí attempted to assassinate the president. He approached Diệm and fired a pistol from close range but missed, hitting the secretary for agrarian reform's left arm. The weapon jammed and security overpowered Tri before he was able to fire another shot. Diệm was unmoved by the incident. The assassination attempt was the desperate response of the Communists to Diệm's relentless anti-Communist policies.

As opposition to Diệm's rule in South Vietnam grew, a low-level insurgency began to take shape there in 1957. Finally, in January 1959, under pressure from southern Việt Cộng cadres who were being successfully targeted by Diệm's secret police (headed by Diệm's brother, Nhu), Hanoi's Central Committee issued a secret resolution authorizing the use of armed insurgency in the South with supplies and troops from the North. On December 20, 1960, under instructions from Hanoi, southern Communists established the Việt Cộng (NLF) in order to overthrow the government of the South. On November 11, 1960, a failed coup attempt against President Ngô Đình Diệm of South Vietnam was led by Lieutenant Colonel Vương Văn Đông and Colonel Nguyễn Chánh Thi of the Airborne Division of the ARVN. There was a further attempt to assassinate Diệm and his family on February 27, 1962, by aerial attack on the presidential palace of Saigon, on the part of two rebel aviators piloting South Vietnamese AD-6 Skyraider aircraft. Diệm and his brother Nhu, the targets of the attack, remained unscathed. One plane was shot down and the pilot arrested, while the other plane took refuge in Cambodia.

In 1962, Diệm established the Strategic Hamlet program as the cornerstone of his counterinsurgency effort.

South Vietnamese "Strategic Hamlets"

From *Cronaca della Guerra del Vietnam, 1961–1975*

On November 13, 1961, Sir Robert G. K. Thompson, British senior advisor in South Vietnam, presented to President Diệm the draft of his plan for the pacification of the Mekong delta area. Thompson's plan, influenced by the victorious British experience in handling the so-called Malayan Emergency, lays the foundations for the future "Strategic Hamlet" program.

March 22–April 22, 1962

"Operation Sunrise" was the first phase of a wide-ranging South Vietnamese counteroffensive against the Việt Cộng, starting from the area of Ben Cat (province of Binh Duong, 50 kilometers from Saigon). The plan is to eliminate the Việt Cộng guerrilla forces by setting up villages that serve as bases for offensive operations and providing the civilians with supplies and facilities to help them defend themselves. This marks the beginning of the "Strategic Hamlet" program, which involves uprooting rural South Vietnamese populations from their original settlements and transferring them to fortified villages defended by local militias. The goal of separating and isolating South Vietnamese farmers from the influence of the Việt Cộng would be achieved only in part, and over fifty villages would soon be infiltrated and occupied by the Việt Cộng after killing or subduing the village leaders. Moreover, once the local militiamen realized that the reinforcements alerted by the South Vietnamese regulars almost never arrived in time, especially after sunset, they would show very little will to fight.

In 1962, the cornerstone of Diệm's counterinsurgency effort—the Strategic Hamlet program (Vietnamese: Ấp Chiến lược), "the last and most ambitious of Diệm's government's nation[-]building schemes," was implemented, calling for the consolidation of 14,000 villages of South Vietnam into 11,000 secure hamlets, each with its own houses, schools, wells, and watchtowers supported by South Vietnamese government. The hamlets were intended to isolate the National Liberation Front (NLF) from the villages, their source for recruiting soldiers, supplies, and information, and to transform the countryside. In the end, because of many shortcomings, the Strategic Hamlet program was not as successful as had been expected and was canceled after the assassination of Diệm. However, according to Miller, the program created a remarkable turnabout in Diệm's regime in their war against communism.

Diệm's favoritism toward Catholics and persecution of South Vietnam's Buddhist majority led to the "Buddhist crisis" of 1963. The violence damaged relations with the United States and other previously sympathetic countries, and his regime lost favor with the leadership of the Army of the Republic of Vietnam (ARVN). On November 1, 1963, the country's leading generals launched a coup d'état with assistance from the CIA. He and his younger brother Nhu initially escaped but were recaptured the following day and assassinated on the orders of Dương Văn Minh, who succeeded him as president. Diệm has been a controversial historical figure in the historiography on the Vietnam War. Some historians have considered him a tool of the United States, while others portrayed him as an avatar of Vietnamese tradition. At the time of his assassination, he was widely considered to be a corrupt dictator.

RELIGIOUS POLICIES AND THE BUDDHIST CRISIS[2]

In a country where surveys of the religious composition estimated the Buddhist majority to be between 70 and 90 percent, Diệm's policies generated claims of religious bias. Diệm was widely regarded by historians as having pursued pro-Catholic policies that antagonized many Buddhists. Specifically, the government was regarded as being biased toward Catholics in public service and military promotions, as well as the allocation of land, business favors, and tax concessions. Diệm also once told a high-ranking officer, forgetting that he was a Buddhist, "Put your Catholic officers in sensitive places. They can be trusted." Many officers in the Army of the Republic of Vietnam converted to Catholicism in the belief that their military prospects depended on it. The distribution of weapons to village self-defense militias intended to repel Việt Cộng guerrillas saw weapons given only to Catholics. Some Buddhist villages converted en masse to Catholicism in order to receive aid or to avoid being forcibly resettled by Diệm's regime, with Buddhists in the army being denied promotion if they refused to convert to Catholicism. Some Catholic priests ran their own private armies, and in some areas forced conversions, looting, shelling, and demolition of pagodas occurred.

The Catholic Church was the largest landowner in the country, and the "private" status imposed on Buddhism by the French required official permission to conduct public Buddhist activities and was never repealed by Diệm. Catholics were also de facto exempt from the corvée labor that the government obliged all citizens to perform; US aid was disproportionately distributed to Catholic-majority villages. The land owned by the Catholic Church was exempt from land reform. Under Diệm, the Catholic Church enjoyed special exemptions in property acquisition, and in 1959, Diệm dedicated his country to the Virgin Mary. The white-and-gold Vatican flag was regularly flown at all major public events in South Vietnam. The newly constructed Huế and Dalat universities were placed under Catholic authority to foster a Catholic-skewed academic environment. Nonetheless,

Diệm had contributed to Buddhist communities in South Vietnam by giving them permission to carry out activities that were banned by French, and supported money for Buddhist schools, ceremonies, and building more pagodas. Among the eighteen members of Diệm's cabinet, there were five Catholics, five Confucians, and eight Buddhists, including a vice president and a foreign minister. Only three of the top nineteen military officials were Catholics.

May 9, 1963. Beginning of the "Buddhist Crisis" in South Vietnam.

From *Cronaca della Guerra del Vietnam, 1961–1975*

South Vietnamese government forces open fire in Huế on Buddhists demonstrating on the day of the anniversary of Buddha, following a ban imposed by President Diệm on flying and parading their flags. Nine were killed and many were injured. Diệm places the blame on the Communists and is never to acknowledge his responsibility.

The law that religious flags could not be waved at public events, but only the South Vietnamese national flag, conceived to develop national sentiment, had been in force for several years and applied to all religious denominations. Until this time, however, the ban had never been strictly enforced, and a few days earlier a Catholic demonstration was the last in which the display of religious flags was tolerated. This apparent, but blatant, inequality of treatment sparked the Buddhist reaction.

May 30, 1963
In total, 350 Buddhist monks demonstrate in Saigon before the National Assembly of South Vietnam and announce a forty-eight-hour hunger strike.

The regime's relations with the United States worsened during 1963, as discontent among South Vietnam's Buddhist majority was simultaneously heightened. In May, in the heavily Buddhist central city of Huế, where Diệm's elder brother was the Catholic archbishop, the Buddhist majority was prohibited from displaying Buddhist flags during Vesak celebrations, commemorating the birth of Gautama Buddha, when the government cited a regulation prohibiting the display of nongovernment flags. A few days earlier, however, white-and-yellow Catholic papal flags flew at the twenty-fifth-anniversary commemoration of Ngô Đình Thục's elevation to the rank of bishop. According to Miller, Diệm then proclaimed the flag embargo because he was annoyed with the commemoration for Thục. However, the ban on religious flags led to a protest led by Thích Trí Quang against the government, which was suppressed by Diệm's forces, and unarmed civilians were killed in the clash. Diệm and his supporters blamed the Việt Cộng for the deaths and claimed that the protesters were responsible for the violence. Although the provincial chief expressed sorrow for the killings and offered to compensate the victims' families, they resolutely denied that government forces were responsible for the killings and blamed the Việt Cộng. According to Diệm, it was the Communists who threw a grenade into the crowd.

From *Cronaca della Guerra del Vietnam, 1961–1975*

June 11, 1963
Self-immolation of Hòa thượng Thích Quảng Đức, a Buddhist monk, who publicly burns himself to death in the street in Saigon in protest against the anti-Buddhist repression and persecution by the Diệm government. In the following months, six other Buddhist monks would follow suit.

July 4, 1963
South Vietnamese general Tran Van Don (Buddhist) contacts the CIA in Saigon to discuss the possibility of a coup against Diệm (Catholic).

August 21, 1963
Raid by the South Vietnamese secret police and special forces, under the orders of Diệm's brother, Ngo Dinh Nhu, against Buddhist pagodas in various parts of the country. The raid results in hundreds of deaths, 1,400 arrests, and the proclamation of martial law.

The Buddhists pushed for a five-point agreement: freedom to fly religious flags, an end to arbitrary arrests, compensation for the Huế victims, punishment for the officials responsible, and religious equality. Diệm then banned demonstrations and ordered his forces to arrest those who engaged in civil disobedience. On June 3, 1963, protesters attempted to march toward the Từ Đàm pagoda. Six waves of ARVN tear gas and attack dogs failed to disperse the crowds. Finally, brownish-red liquid chemicals were doused on praying protesters, resulting in sixty-seven being hospitalized for chemical injuries. A curfew was subsequently enacted.

The turning point came in June, when a Buddhist monk, Thích Quảng Đức, set himself on fire in the middle of a busy Saigon intersection in protest of Diệm's policies; photos of this event were disseminated around the world, and for many people these pictures came to represent the failure of Diệm's government. A number of other monks publicly self-immolated, and the US grew increasingly frustrated with the unpopular leader's public image both in Vietnam and the United States. Diệm used his conventional anti-Communist argument, identifying the dissenters as Communists. As demonstrations against his government continued throughout the summer, the special forces loyal to Diệm's brother, Nhu, conducted an August raid of the Xá Lợi pagoda in Saigon. Pagodas were vandalized, monks were beaten, and the cremated remains of Quảng Đức, which included his heart, a religious relic, were confiscated. Simultaneous raids were carried out across the country, with the Từ Đàm pagoda in Huế looted, the statue of Gautama Buddha demolished, and the body of a deceased monk confiscated. When the populace came to the defense of the monks, the resulting clashes saw thirty civilians killed and two hundred wounded. In all 1,400 monks were arrested, and some thirty were injured across the country. The United States indicated its disapproval of Diệm's administration when ambassador Henry Cabot Lodge Jr. visited the pagoda. No further mass Buddhist protests occurred during the remainder of Diệm's rule.

Madame Nhu Trần Lệ Xuân, Nhu's wife, inflamed the situation by mockingly applauding the suicides, stating, "If the Buddhists want to have another barbecue, I will be glad to supply the gasoline." The pagoda raids stoked widespread public disquiet in Saigon. Students at Saigon University boycotted classes and rioted, which led to arrests, imprisonments, and the closure of the university; this was repeated at Huế University. When high school students demonstrated, Diệm arrested them as well; over a thousand students from Saigon's leading high school, most of them children of Saigon civil servants, were sent to reeducation camps, including, reportedly, children as young as five, on charges of antigovernment graffiti. Diệm's foreign minister, Vũ Văn Mẫu, resigned, shaving his head like a Buddhist monk in protest. When he attempted to leave the country on a religious pilgrimage to India, he was detained and kept under house arrest.

At the same time that the Buddhist crisis was taking place, a French diplomatic initiative to end the war, inspired by Charles de Gaulle, had been launched. The initiative was known to historians as the "Maneli affair," after Mieczysław Maneli, the Polish commissioner to the International Control Commission who served as an intermediary between the two Vietnams. In 1963, North Vietnam was suffering its worst drought in a generation. Maneli conveyed messages between Hanoi and Saigon negotiating a declaration of a ceasefire in exchange for South Vietnamese rice being traded for North Vietnamese coal. On September 2, 1963, Maneli met with Nhu at his office in the Gia Long Palace, a meeting that Nhu leaked to the American columnist Joseph Alsop, who revealed it to the world in his "A Matter of Fact" column in the *Washington Post*. Nhu's purpose in leaking the meeting was to blackmail the United States with the message that if Kennedy continued to criticize Diệm's handling of the Buddhist crisis, Diệm would reach an understanding with the Communists. The Kennedy administration reacted with fury at what Alsop had revealed. In a message to Secretary of State Dean Rusk, Roger Hilsman urged that a coup against Diệm be encouraged to take place promptly, saying that the mere possibility that Diệm might make a deal with the Communists meant that he had to go.

There have been many interpretations of the Buddhist crisis and the immolation of Thích Quảng Đức in 1963. Relating the events to the larger context of Vietnamese Buddhism in the twentieth century and looking at the interactions between Diệm and Buddhist groups, the Buddhist protests during Diệm's regime were not only the struggles against discrimination in religious practices and religious freedom, but also the resistance of Vietnamese Buddhism to Diệm's nation-building policies, centered on a personalist revolution that Buddhists considered a threat to the revival of Vietnamese Buddhist power. Until the end of his life, Diệm, along with his brother Nhu, still believed that their nation building was successful and that they could resolve the Buddhist crisis in their own way, like what they had done with the Hinh crisis in 1954, and the struggle with the Bình Xuyên in 1955.

FOREIGN POLICY

The foreign policy of the Republic of Vietnam (RVN), according to Fishel, "to a very considerable extent," was the policy of Ngo Dinh Diệm himself during this period.[3] He was the decisive factor in formulating foreign policies of the RVN, besides the roles of his adviser Ngô Đình Nhu and his foreign ministers: Trần Văn Độ (1954–55), Vũ Văn Mẫu (1955–63), and Phạm Đăng Lâm (1963), who played subordinate roles in his regime. Nevertheless, since Diệm had to pay much attention to domestic issues in the context of the Vietnam War, foreign policy did not receive appropriate attention from him. Diệm paid more attention to countries that affected Vietnam directly, and he seemed to personalize and emotionalize relations with other nations. The issues that Diệm paid more attention in foreign affairs were the Geneva Accords, the withdrawal of the French, international recognition, the cultivation of the legitimacy of the RVN, and the relations with the United States, Laos (good official relations), Cambodia (complicated relations, especially due to border disputes and minority ethnicities), and especially North Vietnam. Besides, the RVN also focused on diplomatic relations with other Asian countries to secure its international recognition.

Diệm's attitude toward India was not harmonious due to India's non-alignment policy, which Diệm assumed favored communism. It was not until in 1962, when India voted for a report criticizing the Communists for supporting the invasion of South Vietnam, that Diệm eventually re-viewed his opinions toward India. For Japan, Diệm's regime established diplomatic relations for the recognition of war reparations, which led to a reparation agreement in 1959 with the amount of $49 million. Diệm also established friendly relations with non-Communist states, especially South Korea, Taiwan, the Philippines, Thailand, Laos, and the Federation of Malaya, where Diệm's regime shared the common recognition of Communist threats. The RVN established diplomatic relations with Cambodia, India, Burma, Indonesia, Hong Kong, Singapore, Australia, New Zealand, Brazil, Argentina, Mexico, Morocco, and Tunisia.

Regarding the relations with Communist North Vietnam, Diệm maintained total hostility and never made a serious effort to establish any relations with it. In relations with France, as an anticolonialism nationalist, Diệm did not believe in France, and France was always a negative factor in his foreign policy. He also never "looked up on France as a counterweight to American influence."

Concerning relations with the US, although Diệm admitted the importance of the US-RVN alliance, he perceived that the US's assistance to the RVN was primarily serving its own national interest, rather than the RVN's national interest. Keith Taylor adds that Diệm's distrust of the US grew because of its Laotian policy, which gave North Vietnam access to South Vietnam's border through southern Laos. Diệm also feared the escalation of American military personnel in South Vietnam, which threatened his nationalist credentials and the independence of his government. In early 1963, the Ngô brothers even revised their alliance with the US. Moreover, they also disagreed with the US on how to best react to the threat from North Vietnam. While Diệm believed that before opening the political system for the participation of other political camps that military and security matters should be taken into account, the US wanted otherwise and was critical of Diệm's clientelistic government, in which political power was based on his family members and trusted associates. The Buddhist crisis in South Vietnam decreased American confidence in Diệm and eventually led to the coup d'état sanctioned by the US. Ultimately, nation-building politics "shaped the evolution and collapse of the US-Diệm alliance." The different visions in the meanings of concepts—democracy, community, security, and social change—were substantial and were a key cause of the strains throughout their alliance.

As the Buddhist crisis deepened in July 1963, non-Communist Vietnamese nationalists and the military began preparations for a coup. Bùi Diễm, later South Vietnam's ambassador to the United States, reported in his memoirs that General Lê Văn Kim requested his aid in learning what the United States might do about Diệm's government.

Diệm had contacts both in the embassy and with the high-profile American journalists then in South Vietnam, including David Halberstam (*New York Times*), Neil Sheehan (United Press International), and Malcolm Browne (Associated Press).

The coup d'état[4] was designed by a military revolutionary council including ARVN generals led by General Dương Văn Minh. Lt. Col. Lucien Conein, a CIA officer, had become a liaison between the US embassy and the generals, who were led by Trần Văn Đôn. They met each other for the first time on October 2, 1963, at Tân Sơn Nhất airport. Three days later, Conein met with General Dương Văn Minh to discuss the coup and the stance of the US toward it. Conein then delivered the White House's message of American nonintervention, which was reiterated by Henry Cabot Lodge Jr., the US ambassador, who gave secret assurances to the generals that the United States would not interfere.

The coup was chiefly planned by the Vietnamese generals. Unlike the coup in 1960, the plotters of the 1963 coup knew how to gain broad support from other ARVN officer corps. They obtained the support of Generals Tôn Thất Định, Đỗ Cao Trí, and Nguyễn Khánh, as well as the III, II, and I Corps commanders. Only General Huỳnh Văn Cao of IV Corps remained loyal to Diệm.

On November 1, 1963, Conein donned his military uniform and stuffed three million Vietnamese piastres into a bag to be given to General Minh. Conein then called the CIA station and gave a signal indicating that the planned coup against President Diệm was about to start. Minh and his coconspirators swiftly overthrew the government. With only the palace guard remaining to defend Diệm and his younger brother Nhu, the generals called the palace, offering Diệm exile if he surrendered. That evening, however, Diệm and his entourage escaped via an underground passage to Cha Tam Catholic Church in Cholon, where they were captured the following morning. On November 2, 1963, the brothers were assassinated together in the back of an M113 armored personnel carrier with a bayonet and revolver by Captain Nguyễn Văn Nhung, under orders from Minh given while en route to the Vietnamese Joint General Staff headquarters. Diệm was buried in an unmarked grave in a cemetery next to the house of the US ambassador.

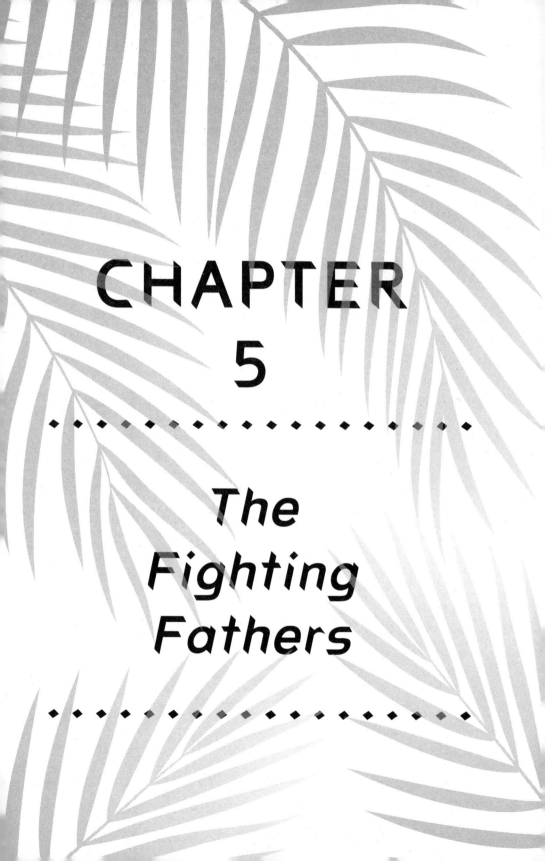

CHAPTER 5

The Fighting Fathers

January 3, 1961

About 15 kilometers from the South Vietnamese village of Bình Hưng, near the peninsula of Ca Mau at the extreme southern tip of Vietnam, around four hundred Việt Cộng (North Vietnamese) attack a group of some ninety defenders, the so-called Sea Swallows, Catholic volunteers of Chinese ethnicity who have gathered around Father Nguyễn Lạc Hóa, one of the Fighting Fathers (militant Catholic priests who supervise and co-ordinate the anti-Communist resistance in their villages and parishes). After a frontal attack and a series of ambushes and counterambushes lasting three days, the Việt Cộng are forced to retreat, reporting 174 deaths against thirty on the side of the Sea Swallows. Following this episode, the CIA station in Saigon would persuade the South Vietnamese special forces and President Diệm to reinforce the village and focus on similar forces throughout the country and the relative backup program. A trilateral South Vietnam–US–ROC (Republic of China, Taiwan) program would also arrange the settlement in the Bình Hưng village of a group of Chinese Nationalist special forces as advisors.

The Fighting Fathers were militant Catholic religious who were involved in the "Stay Behind" program, which, exactly like in Europe, consisted of the creation of a clandestine network capable of launching resistance, partisan, and insurrectionary activities in case of occupation of the territory by forces of the Communist bloc. Obviously, these priests and monks recruited potential resisters from among their own parishioners.

In the coastal region of central South Vietnam, there were three camps managed by the Fighting Fathers, two in Bình Hưng Province and the third in the neighboring (to the north) province of Ninh Thuận, led by one of the most well known of these priests: a certain Brother Bosco, who worked in the Phước Thiện camp, west of Phan Rang.[1]

His "personal army" of parishioners was armed by the CIA from the beginning of December 1961, by CIA agent Jack Benefiel, one of the men of Col. Gilbert Layton, who was head of the MOS (Military Operations Section of the CIA, known by its cover name Combined Studies Division of the MAAG, later MACV) from March 1960 to January 1964. Brother Bosco is mentioned here and there as a Catholic "missionary" or "monk," and one would naturally assume that he was Italian. In actual fact, because St. John Bosco was (and is) very popular among the Catholic minorities of Southeast Asia, many locals named their sons after him, and the nickname Bosco was also very common. It had nothing to do with being Italian;

on the contrary, as in this case, the type of name or nickname used was an indication of their local origins.

Father Nguyễn Lạc Hóa, on the other hand, was a Chinese priest and former officer of the Kuomintang army who took a Vietnamese name when, following the seizing of power by the Communists in mainland China, after being imprisoned in the 1940s, he was moved to Vietnam with three hundred coreligionists. (Douglas Valentine, in his *Phoenix Program*, speaks of two thousand people on his first visit to Laos in 1950. However, here they also encountered persecutions, and so eight years later a Kuomintang agent who worked for the CIA persuaded him to move, along with his followers, to Bình Hưng, in the far south of Vietnam. Some of these may have gone astray before reaching their final destination.)

Almost one million Catholics fled from North to South Vietnam in the 1950s after the decisive takeover by the Việt Minh (by 1955, the number was already 676,384, out of 860,206 civilians fleeing to the South, a total that was to increase significantly over the next few years, without counting the over 124,000 military refugees of the French colonial army, leaving only 833,468 Catholics in the North [statistics from 1964[2]]), and they were more than inclined, partly because of the favorable position obtained thanks to President Diệm, their coreligionist, to oppose the establishment of the Communist regime in the South also. In addition to the ethnic Chinese Sea Swallows, by May 1962 a CIA program known as the Catholic Youth counted as many as 1,100 armed and trained men. This, in a nutshell, represented the concept of the protected and self-defended village that was subsequently developed in the Strategic Hamlet program. William Colby, then head of the CIA station in Saigon, was informed that during a diocesan synod the parish priests had discussed the respective advantages and disadvantages of the Winchester M-2 carbine compared to the Kalashnikov AK-47. In a meeting with Father Hóa at Bình Hưng, Col. Layton, exasperated by the priests' constant requests for more weapons and ammunition, took him by the arm and brought him to see his own armory, which turned out to be full of weapons and ammunition still undelivered to the parishioners. In the years following the fall and death of Diệm and the downsizing of the program of which Father Nguyễn Lạc Hóa had been the leader, the latter moved to Taiwan, where he had been assigned a new parish. The mosaic of ethnic and religious minorities in Vietnam, all more or less resolutely anti-Communist, led to the emergence of decidedly strange situations. In one case, the South Vietnamese special

CIA map. Fighting Fathers locations from Ahern, *CIA and Rural Pacification*. It shows the situation in 1963 for the various counter-insurgency programs. Father Hóa's Sea Swallows are the two orange circles to the extreme south, and the Catholic Youth, at that time also under Father Hóa, was in the single light-blue circle in the same area. The Fighting Fathers in general are the three purple circles in the central-eastern coast, with the easternmost circle being the village of Father Bosco, who was also active farther inland in the smaller villages.

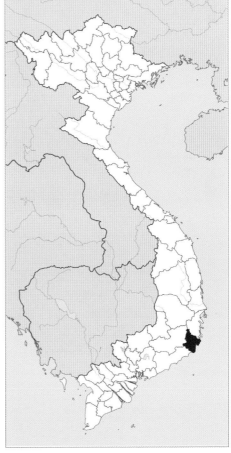

Location of the Vietnamese coastal province of Ninh Thuan, with capital Phan Rang, in which the militiamen of Father Bosco were armed by the CIA

The only known picture of Father Bosco (*at left, in regular cassock*) with the South Vietnamese province chief and his staff. The South Vietnamese were very envious of these activities under American supervision and exercised strict control. *Courtesy Jack Benefiel*

Weapons training for the militiamen of Father Bosco, circa 1963. *Courtesy Jack Benefiel*

Training of the militiamen of Father Bosco, circa 1963. *Courtesy Jack Benefiel*

Another image of weapons training for the irregulars of Father Bosco, circa 1963.
Courtesy Jack Benefiel

Jack Benefiel, the CIA officer responsible for the area, taking care of some children in a village in the area of Father Bosco in 1963. Taking care of the children was the best way to gain the confidence and trust of the locals. As Jack Benefiel put it: "It was always a good way to get the trust of the local boss in the village." *Courtesy Jack Benefiel*

A Việt Cộng with a French submachine gun MAT-49, killed near Father Bosco's village. *Courtesy Jack Benefiel*

Tran van Minh (*at left*) at the time of the Fighting Fathers was the South Vietnamese referent of Jack Benefiel in the zone of Father Bosco. At right is General Ngo Quang Truong, the legendary commander of the South Vietnamese airborne troops.

William Colby in 1965, chief of the Far East Division of the CIA, here at Phuoc Hai, with Colonel Tran Khac Kinh, deputy commander of the 1st Observation Group

Another partial view of the location of the irregular militias in 1963: the two orange circles framed in a rectangle, in the southernmost part, are the home bases of Father Hóa's Sea Swallows. The rectangle in the central-eastern coast shows Father Bosco's village of Phuoc Thien, though he also took care of several internal areas.

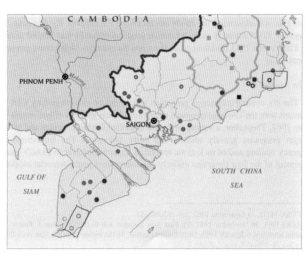

Location of the Ca Mau Province shown on the map of Vietnam, the area where Father Hóa was active

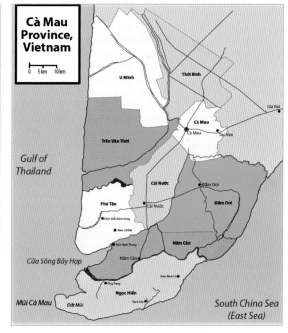

The nine districts of Ca Mau Province

Binh Hung, the protected village of the community led by Father Hóa, in the so-called Hải Yến Special District, created around his leadership, in the Mekong delta.

Sea Swallows and regular South Vietnamese forces waiting for the flag-raising ceremony at Binh Hung. The atmosphere was not particularly martial in this preliminary phase.

Another view of Binh Hung

Another aerial picture of Binh Hung, an ordered and closed fortified village, with perimeter defenses. There was a guard post every 200 yards along the perimeter.

1961. Father Hóa, in black cassock, heads to the flag-raising ceremony in the village.

1961. Father Hóa saluting the flag of South Vietnam. In this image, as in many others, Father Hóa is doing nothing different from all military chaplains.

1961. Father Hóa at the flag raising.

1961. Father Hóa addresses the troops during the flag-raising ceremony.

1961. Again, Father Hóa at the flag raising.

1961. Father Hóa distributing cigarettes to soldiers and militiamen. Cigarettes at the time were part of the care kit or comfort items issued to the military around the world. *Photo by* Life *magazine* *for* Life *magazine*

1961. Father Hóa distributing cigarettes and comfort items to the troops. *Photo by Howard Sochurek for* Life *magazine*

1961. Father Hóa distributing cigarettes and comfort items to the troops. *Photo by Howard Sochurek for* Life *magazine*

1961. South Vietnamese soldiers and Sea Swallows presenting arms to the flag. In the background, Father Hóa on the field altar. Between the American and South Vietnamese flags on top, Newburyport, Massachusetts, reported as the sister city of Binh Hung.

1961. The church of the village of Binh Hung.

1961. Father Hóa celebrating mass.

1961. Father Hóa saying mass to military and civilians.

March 1962. Church of the village of Cai Đài. Father Hóa confesses a soldier. Later he will say Sunday mass for 150 faithful. Note the armed guards in anti–Việt Cộng security duty.

1961. Civilians, mostly women and children, attend the Sunday mass officiated by Father Hóa.

1961. Women and children attending Father Hóa's mass.

1961. Father Hóa in the foreground, on his knees during mass.

The church of Cai Cam, one of the first built in the area by the settlers led by Father Hóa, here in a recent view

Recent view of the
church in Cai Cam

A peaceful image of daily life in Binh Hung. It didn't take too many years before the Sea Swallows were finally defeated, the village being overrun by the Việt Cộng. A disheartened Father Hóa, already deprived of command by the South Vietnamese government, decided to give up, moving first to Saigon and then to Taiwan, where he remained for the rest of his life.

1961. The boats and punts of the settlers in the canal crossing the village of Binh Hung.
Photo by Howard Sochurek

1961. This sign installed in the village reads, more or less, "Long live President Ngo," meaning Ngo Dinh Diệm.

Other buildings in Binh Hung

The main canal crossing Binh Hung.

American advisors visiting the village of Binh Hung

1961. Sea Swallows, the militiamen led by Father Hóa. Behind them, some regular forces, and in the background, the graves of the local cemetery.

1961. Militiamen of Father Hóa leaving on the sampans for a riverine mission. Father Hóa is at the helm of the sampan (*to the low left*), not yet sailed away.

1961. Father Hóa standing, in fatigues and helmet, at the helm of a sampan.

1961. Father Hóa, wearing fatigues, helmet, and glasses, sitting smiling on the handrail on the right, boarding for a mission.

1961. Again, Father Hóa, in the same sequence, just a few seconds afterward. The soldier in the center, with the helmet, is carrying a WWII-vintage Thompson submachine gun.

1961. Father Hóa again (*on the right*), in field uniform and smiling, sitting on the handrail, with helmet and eyeglasses.

1961. Father Hóa on the sampan, leaving for a mission.

Father Hóa, with helmet and glasses, leading his Sea Swallows. His shotgun is not positively identifiable. It's a civilian semiautomatic, a 16-inch-gauge shotgun given to him by an American admirer. But the most-similar models, the Winchester 1400 or the Winchester 1200, vent rib barrel Ted Williams 200, were marketed only some years later.

1961. The Sea Swallows at a funeral ceremony at Binh Hung for a fallen comrade.

The coffin goes on a canal to its final destination.

The coffin carried on a canoe to the burial site

The coffin escorted to the burial site

Again, the coffin escorted to the burial site

The coffin carried for the final part to the burial site

Burial site in the village of Binh Hung. The burials are necessarily made aboveground, given the swampy and marshy nature of the terrain.

The burial. Often this work was handed over to Việt Cộng prisoners detained in the village.

The burial, necessarily done above ground

Burial of the coffin

The graves

The last salute to the fallen, by the Sea Swallows

1964. Father Hóa pauses by the statue of St. Michael during his rounds of the village.

Father Hóa with his parishioners

1962. Binh Hung, flag-raising ceremony.

Col. Ed Lansdale, at the time chief of the CIA military mission in Saigon, meeting President Diệm in 1954

Ed Lansdale, one of the promoters of the activities involving the Fighting Fathers, whose portrait from 1963 is shown here with the rank of major general of the USAF. From 1954 to 1957 he was with the CIA in Saigon, from 1957 to 1963 at the Department of State in Washington, and from 1965 to 1968 again in Saigon, this time at the embassy.

Father Augustine Nguyễn Lạc Hóa

Father Hóa, in plaid shirt, by a C-7 Caribou transport aircraft

Bernard Yoh, Chinese Nationalist, old acquaintance of Father Hóa's, and CIA agent, here communicating during a mission with Father Hóa's militiamen

Photograph of Father Augustine Nguyễn Lạc Hóa, from *Taiwan Review*

Father Hóa with his shotgun. Besides self-defense, he used to use it for hunting hawks, which were a constant threat to the poultry of the villages.

Father Hóa discussing the mission, holding his shotgun

Father Hóa smiling, with his rib-vented 16-inch civilian semiautomatic shotgun

A detail of Father Hóa's civilian semiautomatic shotgun

forces asked for US help to protect the defenders of a village in Dinh Tuong Province of the Mekong delta. When the CIA agent in charge of the case and a South Vietnamese special-forces officer came to inspect the village, they found some sixty volunteers from the Cao Đài sect, a syncretic religion that was established in South Vietnam in the twentieth century. The volunteers were led by a Catholic lay preacher who was a former captain in the French army.

THE HẢI YẾN SPECIAL DISTRICT AND THE "SEA SWALLOWS"

With respect to the community of Father Nguyễn Lạc Hóa (Father Augustinus [or Augustino in the original Vietnamese], often rendered in French as Augustine), the focus of attention of the Americans and of the authorities occurred on January 3, 1961. On that day, 15 kilometers from the South Vietnamese village of Bình Hưng on the Ca Mau Peninsula, at the extreme southern point in Vietnam, some four hundred Việt Cộng attacked around ninety defenders belonging to the so-called Sea Swallows. The Sea Swallows were returning to the village after having escorted Father Hóa to his departure for a trip to Saigon. After a frontal attack and a series of ambushes and counterambushes that lasted three days, the Việt Cộng had to withdraw, having suffered 174 killed against thirty Sea Swallow dead.[3] After that episode, the Saigon CIA station persuaded the South Vietnamese special forces and President Diệm to reinforce the village and to devote attention to similar forces throughout the country and to the program related to them.

On January 5, 1961, two days after the attack, the village of Bình Hưng was visited by Edward Lansdale, who knew Vietnam and Diệm from earlier times. As mentioned, Lansdale, at the time a USAF brigadier general, was no longer in service with the CIA but worked at the Department of Defense. Upon his return to Washington, DC, Lansdale was surprised to learn that the president of the United States himself, John F. Kennedy, had taken an interest in this priest, to the point that he wanted his report to be published in anonymous form in the *Saturday Evening Post*. Lansdale convinced the dictator Diệm to approve large-scale assistance and supplies to the Chinese Catholic village community (arms, food, medicine, and medical assistance). In June 1961, the militia unit received an official name: Self-Defense Corps No. 1001, thus becoming, at least in theory, a unit incorporated into the South Vietnamese army. However, the commander of the unit, who was Father Hóa, refused any formal military rank. He proposed calling the unit the Sea Swallows (in Vietnamese, Hải Yến) instead of the bureaucratic number assigned to it, because the plumage of those birds was reminiscent of a priest's cassock with a white collar, and it also related to birds that ate harmful insects (thus cleaning their territory, as the militiamen wanted to do to the Việt Cộng).

According to other sources, the adoption of the name was due to a romantic reference to the fact that sea swallows return to their place of origin, and that the Chinese felt that they were destined to return to their mother country (continental China) once it had been freed from communism. The militiamen were paid the equivalent of twelve dollars a month (less than the pay of other militiamen in the self-defense units in other areas of the country) and were officially recognized at no more than three hundred men, while the others—another forty combatants in 1961—were paid by donations and with funds provided by personal assets of Nguyễn Lạc Hóa and his friend Bernard Yoh, a former Kuomintang officer who was a CIA collaborator. Several hundred local residents who belonged to ethnic-minority tribes were engaged and involved. Numerous Vietnamese who sought refuge from the Việt Cộng also joined the community. In two years the population of Bình Hưng quadrupled. A market, a school, and a hospital were opened. Because of these activities, by mid-1961, Father Hóa and Bernard Yoh, who had spent all their own money for the needs of the inhabitants of Bình Hưng, had run up debts of more than $100,000. Some aid, however, was provided by American charity organizations, both Catholic and lay.

The capability and the courage that they had shown in the field, in addition to their favorable position that they enjoyed as Catholics with President Diệm, their coreligionist (some sources refer to Diệm as a "fellow seminarian" of Father Hóa, but this, in my opinion, is gossip without any real basis), naturally made the Sea Swallows among the leading candidates for American military assistance. Nevertheless, as civilian militiamen, they did not have access to the US Military Assistance Program. William Colby, at the time the CIA station chief in Saigon, remedied that by sending a special-forces team (Green Berets) that had been assigned locally to the CIA for missions of this type. A fourteen-man "A" Team (ODA, or Operational Detachment Alpha) was parachuted into Bình Hưng in early January 1962. Colby and South Vietnamese colonel Tung (head of the

Vietnamese special forces) had observed the drop of this team, probably from a light aircraft flying in the area (Colonel Trung, a faithful follower of Diệm, would later be assassinated along with his brother Trieng during the November 2, 1963, coup). The inhabitants of the village had also built a landing strip, and resupply flights by twin-engine de Havilland Canada DHC-4 Caribou aircraft soon began.

In January 1962, when Bình Hưng was visited for the first time by a Western journalist, Father Hóa's "army" numbered about a thousand men, of whom six hundred were Chinese who had had military experience with the Kuomintang; the rest were Vietnamese. In the space of two years, they eliminated approximately five hundred Việt Cộng, themselves losing only twenty-seven men, most of whom were victims of mines and explosive booby traps. Over a hundred Việt Cộng prisoners were detained at Bình Hưng (where they were employed mainly in working five or six hours a day in the rice paddies, except for Sundays, and then were made to listen to two hours of political indoctrination); after a certain time, most of the prisoners were released to return to their own villages, from which they were often torn and enrolled by force by the Việt Cộng, while others opted to remain in Father Hóa's community.

Father Hóa had asked for the agreement of his superiors in the Catholic hierarchy for his activities; the religious authorities did not give him official permission, but neither did they pose any objections, because they were aware that the lives of many people depended on the leadership and experience (including military) of Father Hóa. At the end of 1963, the Sea Swallows had managed to place an area of 220 square kilometers under their control. Of the 18,000 inhabitants of that territory, only 3,700 were Catholic. Father Hóa collaborated with local Buddhist leaders and with the Cao Đài syncretic sect, saying, "In conducting these operations, we can't make any distinctions between Buddhists and Catholics. If we are fighting for freedom, it means that we believe that all people should be free."

The ranks of the Sea Swallows were strengthened when Father Hóa began to recruit other Chinese Catholics in Cho Lon, Saigon's Chinatown. The origins and the Chinese language of the Sea Swallows provided the opportunity for the Chinese Nationalist government of Taiwan to get involved in the fight against the North Vietnamese. In April 1962, the resulting United States–South Vietnam–Taiwan trilateral agreement led to a Taiwanese special-forces team being sent to Bình Hưng (called Ping Hsing by the Chinese), joining South Vietnam and American special forces. As happened with the CIDG (Civilian Irregular Defense Group units, the militia groups in the Central Highlands and in the mountains, recruited among the *montagnards*), the presence of South Vietnamese special forces was aimed at underscoring control by the Saigon government. However, Father Hóa, accustomed to dealing with political authorities, quickly gained the support and trust of Lieutenant Chương, who was Colonel Tung's "man in the field." Father Hóa was able to bring Lieutenant Chương over to his side to the point that a CIA agent observed that Chương now looked more like a Sea Swallow than he did a South Vietnamese officer or functionary.

By midsummer 1962, the Saigon CIA station had delivered 1,400 weapons of various types to the Sea Swallows, and the number of volunteers trained by the joint American-Taiwanese team was pushing two thousand men.[4]

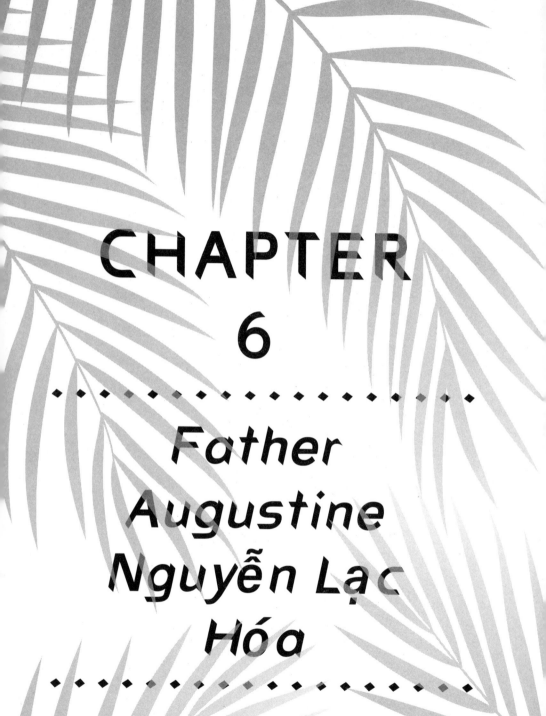

CHAPTER 6

Father Augustine Nguyễn Lạc Hóa

Let us take a look at Father Hóa's personal history. He was the founder and person responsible for the anti-Communist area called the Hải Yến Special District on the Ca Mau Peninsula, at the extreme southern point of Vietnam, a historically Việt Cộng stronghold. Father Augustine Nguyễn Lạc Hóa was born on August 28, 1908, with the name of Chen I-cheng to a family of fishermen in the Leichow (Leizhou) Peninsula in the Chinese province of Guangdong (Canton), near the Gulf of Tonkin. He had two sisters (one adoptive and one blood) and three brothers: Thanh, Phat, and Ngia. At the age of fifteen he entered the Pakhoi seminary (now known as Beihai), the seat of a Catholic mission, in the southern province of Guangxi, and from 1927 studied at the papal college (Collège General) at Pulau Tikus on the Penang Peninsula in Malaysia. He later to returned to China. He was ordained as a priest in Hong Kong on July 17, 1935. His religious name was Augustinus (sometimes Italianized to Augustino in the original Vietnamese, or often Frenchified as Augustine). He served as an assistant of the Leizhou Peninsula parish. In spring of 1939, as the first-born male of the family, and even though he was a priest, he was drafted, taking part in the Sino-Japanese war (1937–45). It should not be forgotten that China, not being traditionally tied to any of the great monotheist religions, had no provisions for chaplains in the army. Thus, Father Hóa was trained as an officer and in guerrilla warfare. At the time of Japan's surrender, he had reached the rank of major. He had fought against both the Sino-Communists and the Japanese in the area called Shih-Wan-Ta-Shan ("A Hundred Thousand Great Mountains"), on the border between Kwangtung (Guangdong) and Kwangshi (Guangxi). Despite his desire to return to his priestly duties, he was not discharged, remaining in service for another three and a half years fighting against Mao's Communists, and was promoted to lieutenant colonel.

Finally discharged from military service in June 1949, he was able to return to Pakhoi, where he was charged to run the hospital and orphanage. When, on December 5, 1949, Pakhoi was occupied by the Chinese Communists, Hóa left the city and with the consent of the bishop moved to Indochina, then still under French rule. Soon after, however, he received a letter from the bishop, who ordered him to return to Pakhoi. In answer to his question as to why he should return there, the bishops' reply was "To die." Father Hóa returned to Pakhoi without delay, where he was immediately arrested as a "reactionary" by the Communist authorities.

Following a three-day trial, he was imprisoned but was later placed under house arrest, because the Communists hoped to draw them to their side to use him for propaganda purposes (see the future Chinese Patriotic Church, or the Protestant church of the Three Independences), or to exhibit him as proof of religious freedom in China. On December 16, 1950, after a year and four days, with the aid of his parishioners he was able to escape in a boat and reach northern Vietnam. He wrote several letters to Mao Tse Tung, delivered through acquaintances in Paris, in which he displayed his hostility to Communist ideology, which by now characterized him.

Around him, by that time having adopted a Vietnamese name—that of Nguyễn Lạc Hóa—he began to gather a community of Chinese refugees. In six months, with his help, about 450 families (2,174 people, including former military personnel, men, women, and children) left the areas of China that were under Communist control and established themselves in Vietnam. At the time, the situation in northern Vietnam was problematic, with French colonial control increasingly threatened by the Việt Minh partisans, and several religious sects agitating with their own armed for-mations. After seeking a more peaceful place, having visited Laos and Thailand, Hóa finally decided to move his followers to Cambodia, with the aid of French authorities. For seven years, the refugees established themselves in Kratie Province, mainly working on local plantations, leading a rather miserable life. The political situation, however, did not take much time to become complicated and then deteriorate. In 1956, Father Hóa put some money aside for a trip around the world, which lasted six months and brought him to twenty-five countries, but without finding an adequate place of refuge for his two thousand refugees. In 1958, when Cambodia, now independent of French protection, officially recognized the People's Republic of China, Father Hóa's community perceived the move as a sign of danger (Prince Sihanouk, then the Cambodian prime minister, was going through one of his recurring pro-Maoist periods) and decided to move elsewhere. Those who were able immigrated to Taiwan, while others, thanks to Father Hóa's action (as suggested by Bernard Yoh, a former Kuomintang officer who worked for the CIA) and his personal contacts with Diệm, were able to settle in the Mekong delta in South Vietnam; about 450 people arrived on March 17, 1959, and others joined them later. The chosen area was a swampy area below sea level, around 700 square kilometers, and was marked by Việt Cộng bases.

Under Father Hóa's leadership, the colonists built their new settlement themselves. With the support of the Diệm government, in Cai Cam and Bình Hưng, each family received 3 hectares (7.4 acres) of land, a buffalo, two water jars, a boat, rice for six months, and material to build a house. In each of the two villages, a large church was built (the one in Cai Cam still exists and is indeed large for the area in which it was located), with a statue of the Madonna and a cross.

The scale of these settlements grew significantly with the influx of 120 ethnic Chinese minority families. With a population that was under control and well governed, as well as organized and trained so as to be able to constitute a military area, Father Hóa asked President Diệm to approve setting up a special zone, with its center, based in the village of Bình Hưng (which the Chinese called Ping Hsing), called the Hải Yến Special Zone or Special District (in Vietnamese, Hải Yến means "sea swallow" or "swift").

From 1959 to 1960, Father Hóa was allowed to form militia platoons, was designated by Diệm as the commander of the Hải Yến zone, and was given the military rank equivalent to major. The Chinese settlers busied themselves with agriculture (achieving notable results in cultivating rice) and in organizing their self-defense forces against Việt Cộng attacks.

Initially, settlers had only clubs and six hand grenades to defend themselves. In December 1959, they received twelve old French rifles. Father Hóa sought to find time to procure other weapons. In June 1960 the village received another ninety French rifles, two submachine guns, and twelve pistols from the South Vietnamese authorities. Settlers between eighteen and forty-five years of age were armed and received a brief but intense period of training, lasting two months, for men and women. On November 19, they were organized as No. 1001 Group and took an oath to fight the Việt Cộng until death (as noted above, another source reports June 1961 as the official date of the unit's founding).

The military zone was an area of about 80 hectares (198 acres), surrounded by a protective wall 1.20 meters (3.9 feet) high, with a barbed-wire barrier. Inside the base lived a civilian and military community organized along rather modern lines. There was an airstrip, a headquarters, the residence of American advisors, a church, an area dedicated to the families, a detention center for captured Việt Cộng, a hospital, and an armory. Over time, electric lights and a water supply were introduced and a small stadium was built. A model house was designed by Father Hóa and built under his supervision, to demonstrate that even in swampy areas it was possible to build adequate housing. Basic instruction was given to about three hundred children of school age.

In December 1960, a Việt Cộng unit infiltrated the village, trying to raise the Communist flag in place of the South Vietnamese flag, but he was discovered and killed. From that moment on, the Việt Cộng initiated a series of attacks both by day as well as by night, usually on a biweekly basis, suffering losses that were not indifferent. [*Note*: In the six largest attacks at the time, the Việt Cộng suffered losses of eight to one, a sort of halfway mark between the proportion suffered by the North Vietnamese against the Americans and that suffered against the South Vietnamese regular army.]

The Sea Swallows also carried out intelligence activities; members of the village who pretended to be Việt Cộng businessmen converted to Father Hóa's cause infiltrated among their adversaries to gain as much knowledge as they could about enemy movements.

The village peasants called Father Hóa "the Old Man" as a sign of affection and reverence. Many of the captured Việt Cộng were won over by Father Hóa's personality and joined the Sea Swallows. Three meals a day and decent quarters were probably other inducements that helped convert Việt Cộng prisoners.

After the previously reported attack on January 3, 1961 attack, it was decided to reinforce the settlement's defenses. In various increments, the inhabitants of Bình Hưng received additional arms and ammunition from the South Vietnamese government. They were also trained in the use of knives and hand-to-hand combat. The Bình Hưng militia squads passed from the simple self-defense role to active action against the Việt Cộng.

The village was well protected. Defenses consisted of guard posts, barbed wire, and outer minefields to prevent human wave attacks, which were typical of the North Vietnamese. A canal crossed through the village from east to west (a sort of "via principalis" of a Roman military camp) and linked it to outer roads.

Progressively, other American humanitarian aid agencies took advantage of the security conditions in the so-called Hải Yến Special District. Col. Gilbert Layton, who from March 1960 to January 1964 was the chief of the MOS (Military Operations Section of the CIA, a cover designation for the Combined Studies Division of the MAAG, later to become MACV, the US military command in Vietnam) and was also the supervisor of CIA operations with the Fighting Fathers, found the continuous, insistent requests by Father Hóa for more supplies and weapons to be irritating, however. Perhaps conditioned by past restrictions, Hóa acted as though there were never enough weapons for his small army, and he implored each of the numerous American visitors to intercede to help him fill the presumed shortages, especially weapons. These entreaties regularly landed on Gilbert Layton's desk. Once, when Father Hóa began the litany during a meeting in Bình Hưng, Layton took the priest by the arm and led him to inspect the armory, which turned out to be full of arms and equipment that had not yet been distributed to his militiamen.

On December 31, 1962, the members of the Combat Youth in the various provinces that had been armed and trained by the CIA to fight the Việt Cộng under the leadership of the Fighting Fathers reached a total of more than 4,500.

In 1961, Father Hóa's Hải Yến Special District had between 1,200 and 1,800 combat-ready men and women. There were three hundred armed women in the village, and of those, seventy were trained to use heavy machine guns.

In reality, of the various strategic villages installed in South Vietnam as part of the American strategy, only those of Father Hóa's Sea Swallows had had repeated successes against the Việt Cộng.[1]

In addition to being the commander of the military force and governor of the Sea Swallows, Father Hóa was the superintendent of the hospital and the principal of the high school and in 1964 had been presented with the Magsaysay Award, a very high Philippine award for public service.

Between 1963 and 1965 the Sea Swallows captured more than two hundred Việt Cộng, including cadres and agents, including several women.

In 1965, the Sea Swallows (Hải Yến) Special District grew to ten combat groups with 138 men each, organized into three units consisting of three squads. Armament had increased to include artillery, mortars, and machine guns deployed in the village and its surrounding area.

The field uniform was olive drab with a golden sea swallow tab on the collar. No rank insignia was worn on the uniforms. Pay, work, and responsibilities were assigned on an equal basis. Among themselves, the male fighters called themselves brothers, and the females, sisters.

A special task force was responsible for training, which included the use of weapons, physical training, psychological warfare, assessment of intelligence, telecommunications, and first-aid techniques.

In September 1961, the US Marines sent a seven-man team to Bình Hưng to study the problematic tactics connected with its defense. After this, three American advisors were sent to supervise the building of an airstrip and of other defensive works and to conduct meteorological research. Because of its isolated position, supplies had to be delivered by air, and the new airstrip could handle C-123 and C-46 aircraft, which were much larger than the Caribou, the efficient but small STOL (short takeoff and landing) aircraft that had necessarily been used until then.

The town of Hyannis Port, Massachusetts, President Kennedy's summer residence, declared its twinning with Bình Hưng as a sign of recognition for the activity it was carrying out. Of a population of about two thousand inhabitants in Bình Hưng, 90 percent were of Chinese origin.

The operational problem was that Bình Hưng (Ping Hsing as it was called by the Chinese and Vietnamese) was too large to be defended completely and at the same time was too small to act as a strategic base for long-range operations throughout the province. Morale, however, remained high for a long time. Following a visit to Taiwan in 1965, Father Hóa said, "For fourteen years we were like wandering orphans. I now have reported [to the refugees in South Vietnam] the warmth and attention of our mother country. We are no longer alone in picking up rifles against the Việt Cộng." Father Hóa received encouragement and the personal appreciation of President Chiang Kai-shek.

As mentioned earlier, these units were supported and trained by the so-called US Special Forces A-teams. In 1967, a team of five American military personnel from MACV, designated Team 59 and led by Henry Dagenais, replaced US Special Forces A-team 411, which until that time had supported the Hải Yến area. Unfortunately, Father Hóa was replaced as military commander by South Vietnamese officers of dubious ability, and with little control over the militiamen, leaving the priest in the role of advisor and intermediary. The mutual mistrust between Chinese and Vietnamese, as well as the lack of tactical and logistic support for the Sea Swallows, did the rest.

Henry "Hank" Dagenais (later colonel), who was the MACV senior advisor for the area from September 1967 to September 1968, with his five MACV men, describes the situation well: "At that time (1967), the south Vietnamese commander, a certain Major Nuoc, was a corrupt individual who shook down the local peasants, demanding 'taxes' from the village inhabitants and threatening to open fire on them with 105 mm artillery if the did not pay up." However, in the end the Americans had him removed and replaced by a captain who had been the commander of a South Vietnamese ranger battalion: he was a man of completely different cut, defined by the Americans as "a straight arrow"; that is to say, incorruptible.

A brother of Father Hóa's was actively present in the area and was nicknamed "Mr. Niep" or "Nip" and was a lieutenant in the South Vietnamese air force. He had previously acted as a CIA agent in the North. Initially, he was responsible for the village slated for settlement by Catholics on the beach north of Square Bay, which was also in the Hải Yến District area. He was familiar with the southern tip of the Ca Mau Peninsula, including Việt Cộng hiding places, better than anyone else, to the point that in later years, in 1969–70, it was he who presented premission briefings to the three platoons of US Navy SEALs from the American base at Solid Anchor on the Cau Lon River; it also was he, in substance, who was an "advisor" to the Americans. Officially he was one of the company commanders, but in reality he was the leader of all the Chinese militiamen in the area. All orders given by the new South Vietnamese commander had to have his blessing; otherwise it was simply ignored. Father Hóa himself distrusted the South Vietnamese. On one occasion, when he was leaving the Hải Yến area to return to Cho Lon (the Chinese district of Saigon), he told Dagenais that if they were in danger of being overwhelmed or captured, it would be better to turn to his brother rather than to the South Vietnamese headquarters.

According to official figures provided by Vietnamese Communist authorities, the Sea Swallows alone killed 1,657 Việt Cộng, but that figure may be incomplete. Conscious of the danger and the obstacle that this community constituted, the Việt Cộng took measures to inflict heavy blows on the militiamen to decimate them. The Việt Cộng had to—at all costs—eliminate this very dangerous spine from their side, in an area in which they had previously owned, so that after a certain time they attacked the "Sea Swallows" without letup, inflicting heavy losses. Progressively, after Diệm's death, the assumption of command by South Vietnamese officers who were not always respected or up to the task, and the progressive decrease of attention and resources dedicated to this program throughout Vietnam, led to the decline and ultimately to the end of these experiments. The central government in Saigon had always looked upon these activities as suspect, while on the American side, with General Westmoreland and his vision that was sharply focused on large-scale war and the ill-disguised contempt for these operations and programs that were defined as "the other war," in a pejorative sense, everything slowly came to an end, rendering in vain all the efforts and results that had been achieved. Beginning in 1964, all of the South Vietnamese regional forces were integrated into the South Vietnamese regular army, or ARVN (Army of the Republic of Vietnam) and placed under the control of the Joint General Staff in Saigon.

From mid-1966, at the time of the greatest number of Catholic militias and their affiliates, the Việt Cộng U Minh 2 Battalion (located in the area near the U Minh forest) had set ambushes and seriously damaged or destroyed all the main units of the so-called Hải Yến District. Following these defeats, the authorities in Saigon ordered the abandonment of the Hải Yến area, moving government units to areas more under their control. This evolution of the situation, begun after Diệm's death, had discouraged and even disappointed Father Hóa, who moved to Saigon to dedicate himself to purely priestly duties.

Around 1973, because of his advanced age and the pessimism that had pervaded him because of the corruption and repressive attitude of the Saigon regime, Father Hóa now looked upon anti-Communist activity in Vietnam as a dead-end street and asked to be transferred to Taiwan, where he was greeted and was assigned a new parish, and where he died in 1989.

BIOGRAPHY

The following is taken from information contained in the Ramon Magsaysay Award Foundation documentation, in describing the character and the reasons of the assignation of the award to Father Hóa in 1964.

AUGUSTINE NGUYEN LAC HOA was born in the village of Chuc San, Fang Cheng Hsien, near the Gulf of Tongking and the Vietnam border in Kwangtung Province (today's Guangdong), China[,] on August 28, 1908. The eldest son of a Cantonese fisherman, he was named YUN LOC-FA, or in Mandarin YUAN LO-HUA. Under his father's tutelage he acquired his first skill of handling small boats. Graduating from middle school at the age of 15, he returned to help his father in fishing but, after twice losing his way at sea, decided to become a priest. That fall he entered Saint Therese Seminary for diocesan priests at Pakhoi, where he studied for four years. In 1927, he was sent to the Pontifical College in Penang, Malaya, to complete his formal training for the priesthood. In the winter of 1933 he returned to Pakhoi to teach at Saint Therese Seminary and serve as helper to the parish priest. Ordained on July 17, 1935, in Hong Kong, he returned again to Pakhoi to teach at the Seminary until January 1937, when he was sent to Suikai Hsien on the Luichow Peninsula as assistant to the parish priest.

There Father YUN found himself serving as curate in a district controlled by Wong Lo-dai, a former schoolmate who had become a notorious South China river pirate. Soon after his arrival, when one of the pirate's men took a fancy to his bicycle and confiscated it, the priest protested and told the thief to take him to the presence of Wong Lo-dai. Recalling their school days[,] Wong Lo-dai feted Father YUN and asked him to stay a week. The priest demurred to avoid anxiety on the part of the parish and the authorities but left the following day with Wong Lo-dai's assurance of personal safety for himself and his parishioners. Later Father YUN admitted three of the pirate chieftain's sons into his Holy Trinity School, keeping their identities secret at their father's request.

In the spring of 1939, when China was at the lowest ebb in her struggle against the Japanese, the National Government [*sic*] conscripted the eldest sons of every family into the army to fight the invaders. Being an eldest son[,] Father YUN was one of the draftees and, there being no chaplain system in the Chinese army, his religious career was involuntarily suspended when he was inducted as a private in the regular combat ranks. A week later when interviewing officers found him educated, he was sent to Toc San in the nearby mountains for special guerrilla training which would qualify him as an officer.

Escaping in late 1950 and early 1951 from Communist persecution of Roman Catholics in Kwangtung Province (today's Guangdong) in South China, Father AUGUSTINE NGUYEN LAC HOA and 2,100 of his parishioners lived precariously for eight years in Cambodia. In 1956, the priest searched in 25 countries for a more permanent solution for his people but found only sympathy and no answer to their problem. Forced again to move by communist guerrilla harassment and finally Cambodian recognition of Communist China, many of the stateless refugees sought sanctuary on their own in the new Republic of South Vietnam. A few who could afford the long voyage left for Taiwan. Learning from the priest of their plight, the government of South Vietnam offered to the remaining 450 facilities to migrate, citizenship[,] and a homestead.

On March 17, 1959, Father HOA and his weary flock arrived at Binh Hung, the remote place on the southernmost Ca Mau Peninsula where they had permission to settle. Swampy, mosquito-infested and imperiled by guerrillas entrenched in surrounding mangrove forests, it was barely habitable, but the land was fertile and fish were plentiful in waterways crisscrossing the delta.

In three months of relentless toil that spared no adult or child, a village was raised above the flooded land and the first rice crop planted. The guerrilla-wise priest, himself a former soldier, also drilled every man to be an aggressive fighter. When the Viet Cong struck, the villagers fought back, armed only with fishing knives and wooden staves. With the few weapons then supplied by the government, the defenders suffered losses but never defeat in the frequent raids and ambushes that followed. Father HOA taught them no battle could be won by standing still; day and night patrols moved out[,] learning every place for ambush or hiding and engaging the enemy on his own ground.

The fighting spirit of the little band earned government recognition as a Village Self-Defense Corps, qualifying it for military aid. Refugee Chinese Nationalist soldiers, Montagnards from the central highlands, Nung from the north, and local Vietnamese were recruited to join the defenders. Urgently needed supplies began to arrive regularly by helicopter. Government agencies, Catholic Relief Services, CARE, and others helped. In three years, Vietnamese moving in from outlying farms for protection swelled the population of the village and adjoining hamlets to over 1,500.

As military commander without rank for Hải Yến Special District, the priest worked closely with Buddhist and Cao-Đàist leaders—whose adherents were most numerous in the area—to promote security measures in villages. Though the Viet Cong were not eliminated, his Corps of Sea Swallows—by late 1963 numbering more than 1,000—extended relative security over 200 square kilometers to 18,000 inhabitants.

This year [1964], when the military command was given to regular army officers, Father HOA welcomed the change. Now 56, he devotes his energies to his spiritual duties and schools, and serves as adviser-chaplain to the Sea Swallows, admonishing any who tire of the long struggle: "For our freedom, if we are tired, we cannot be free."

In electing Father AUGUSTINE NGUYEN LAC HOA to receive the 1964 Ramon Magsaysay Award for Public Service, the Board of Trustees recognizes "his extraordinary valor in defense of freedom, strengthening among a beleaguered people the resolution to resist tyranny."

FATHER HÓA'S RESPONSE

There are wonderful surprises that come our way, at one time or another, in our life. And to me this prestigious award is the greatest and most wonderful surprise of all.

I am here today to receive this great honor of the Magsaysay Award, not on my behalf, but on behalf of the men and women who have fought, and are still fighting, under the insignia of the Sea Swallows. The great benefit of this award will go to the Sea Swallows[,] who are enduring great hardships to maintain tranquility and security for the thousands of inhabitants in our swampy area. But the glory of this award should go to no one else but 203 Sea Swallows who have offered their lives voluntarily to the cause of freedom and justice for all.

As for myself, I am only a simple priest who tries to do his duty in administering to the people of my area. Normally, a priest would simply administer to the spiritual needs of his flock. But in the area where we are, we have to do more.

There are those who have suggested that we should be like the early Christians, to allow ourselves to be killed for our faith. But experience has taught us that communism does not allow us the luxury of martyrdom. Yes, I can tell you from personal experience. I have tried. I spent over 12 months in their jails. The god-hating communists are not satisfied by merely taking our bodies, what they want is our souls.

Fighting really is the minor part of the struggle against communism. The most important part is the struggle for the minds, the hearts, and the souls of the people? All people, especially the communists. And it is precisely on this premise that your great President Magsaysay was able to defeat the Hukbalahap rebellion.

Many have asked me, if that is the case, why are we not winning in Vietnam? My answer is simple. The misplacement of the order of importance. The Magsaysay Way is winning the people first, winning the war second. I am afraid in Vietnam today the order is reversed.

I can talk plainly like this because I am a soldier as well as a priest. Weapons are important. Fighting is necessary in order to protect the people from being physically harmed by the armed communists. But arms are useful only for defensive purposes. Our offense is to rely solely on winning the people, because as soon as the people understand what communism means, and as soon as they have faith in our ability to protect them, and as soon as they have confidence in our integrity, the battle is won.

When fought as a conventional war, we really have no chance to win. How can we explain to a mother when her child is burned by napalm? And how can we expect a young man to fight for us when his aged father was killed by artillery fire? Indeed, how can we claim to be with the people when we burn their homes simply because those houses happen to be in the Viet Cong–controlled territory?

You may say that it is easy for me as a priest to think of love above war, but facts have proved that love is the only way for us to win. It is the only way for us to survive.

In conclusion, I want to extend our deep, deep appreciation for the great honor and benefit you have bestowed upon us. May God bless the people of the Philippines. It is my sincere hope that you will continue to promote the Magsaysay Way, the only way that the world can be peaceful and free.

FROM THE *NEW YORK TIMES*, SEPTEMBER 1, 1964

MANILA, Aug. 31 (UPI)—A Roman Catholic soldier-priest, whose parish lies in guerrilla[-]infested South Vietnamese territory, charged today that cruelty was being used in the war against the Communists.

The priest, the Rev. Augustine Nguyen Lac Hoa, spoke at the presentation of six 1964 Ramon Magsaysay Awards for outstanding service to Asia.

He said South Vietnamese leaders were placing priority on winning the war rather than winning the people.

Guests who had previously attended the annual presentation ceremonies said this was one of the strongest speeches.

The prizes were established in 1957 in honor of the President of the Philippines, who had died in an air crash. Each award includes $10,000 in cash, a gold sunburst medal[,] and a citation.

Father Hoa won his award for "extraordinary valor in defense of freedom." He was specifically cited for work in building a settlement out of swamplands in Binh Hung, South Vietnam, after fleeing from Communist China in 1950.

He organized, trained[,] and commanded the Army of Sea Swallows, a group that resisted the Viet Cong within the settlement.

Emphasis "Misplaced"

Father Hóa said his award would go "to the Sea Swallows, who are enduring great hardships to maintain tranquility and security for the thousands of inhabitants in our swampy area."

Paying tribute to the late Philippine president, he said Mr. Magsaysay had successfully fought the Filipino Communist Hukbalahaps with a dynamic program that won "the minds, the hearts[,] and souls of people—all people, especially the Communists."

He added: "Many have asked me, 'If that is the case, why are we not winning in Vietnam?' My answer is simple: the misplacement of the order of importance. The Magsaysay way is winning the people first, winning the war second. I am afraid in Vietnam today, the order is reversed."

"I can talk plainly like this because I am a soldier as well as priest," he said. "Fighting is necessary in order to protect the people from being physically harmed by the armed Communists. But arms are useful only for defensive purposes.

"Our offense is to rely solely on winning the people, because as soon as the people have understood what Communism means, and as soon as they have faith in our ability to protest that, and as soon as they have confidence in our integrity the battle is won."

Known as "Fighting Priest"

Father Hoa, who is called the Fighting Priest, may be more experienced in guerrilla warfare than most of the Communists against whom he has waged war for six years.

The 56-year-old priest began his study of tactics in China in the long struggle first against the Japanese and later against the Chinese Communists.

He was originally named Yuan Lo-wha, a third-generation member of a Chinese Catholic family in Kwantung Province (Guangdong).

With the collapse of Japan, Father Hoa hoped to take up his priestly duties once more, but the defeat and expulsion of the Chinese Nationalists stood in his way. He escaped to North Vietnam in 1950 and a year later left that French colony for temporary refuge in Cambodia as the spiritual leader of 2,000 Chinese Catholics.

In 1958, when Cambodia recognized Communist China, the refugee colony dispersed under Government pressure. Most of the group fled to Taiwan or to South Vietnam.

The remnants of Father Hoa's band were permitted to settle in the swampy, remote[,] and underpopulated southernmost area of the Ca Mau Peninsula.

It was there, at Binh Hung, that they began the struggle against the Communist guerrillas who had held it almost from the moment in 1954 when the French left Vietnam.

Employing his long experience in China, Father Hoa began to weld an informal army.

While building his village and fortifying it against attacks, Father Hoa trained his growing band in the arts of counterattack, often striking as the guerrillas were preparing assaults and outmaneuvering the Viet Cong in frequent clashes.

Attacks on his village became less frequent as the Communists were caught in raid after raid at a disadvantage.

Father Hoa's responsibility covered 22 villages in the Hải Yến Special District of An Xuyen Province. He received significant if irregular help from the United States. Of his efforts[,] Gen. Lyman L. Lemnitzer[,] then the chairman of the Joint Chiefs of Staff, said during a visit to Binh Hung in 1962: "This is an example for the entire Free World to emulate. Against this kind of courage Communism simply cannot win."

The motives of the Vietnamese Government for the move were unclear. Only a few weeks before, Father Hoa had received full assurances of support from Maj. Gen. Nguyen Khanh, then Premier. Some Americans thought that the order had originated with army officers well below Premier Khanh and that personal jealousies might have been involved.

Complete Version:

SAIGON'S TACTICS SCORED BY PRIEST
SEPT. 1, 1964
MANILA, Aug. 31 (UPI)—A Roman Catholic soldier-priest, whose parish lies in guerrilla-infested South Vietnamese territory, charged today that cruelty was being used in the war against the Communists.

The priest, the Rev. Augustine Nguyen Lac Hoa, spoke at the presentation of six 1964 Ramon Magsaysay Awards for outstanding service to Asia.

He said South Vietnamese leaders were placing priority on winning the war rather than winning the people.

"When it is fought as a conventional war, we have no chance to win," Father Hoa said after receiving his award.

He added: "How can we explain to a mother when her child is burned by napalm? And how can we expect a young man to fight for us when his aged father was killed by artillery fire? Indeed, how can we claim to be with the people when we burn their homes simply because those houses happen to be in the Viet Cong–controlled territory?"

FROM THE *NEW YORK TIMES*, APRIL 28, 1964

SAIGON REPLACES "FIGHTING PRIEST"

PETER GROSE; Special to the *New York Times*, APRIL 28, 1964
SAIGON, South Vietnam, April 27—A Roman Catholic priest whose irregular military methods have carved out a safe haven for his followers in the Communist-dominated Ca Mau Peninsula has been deprived of the command of his private army.

A major of the South Vietnamese Army has been named commander of Father Hoa's area, called the Hai Yen, or "Sea Swallows," sector.

The sector, near the Gulf of Siam, has long been a showplace, an example of what highly motivated counterinsurgent operations could accomplish against the Communist guerrillas.

The appointment of the commander, Maj. Chương Chinh Quay , came quietly about 10 days ago. Father Hoa, who came here from China, confirmed today that he had in effect been supplanted and might have to leave Vietnam.

American officials who have strongly supported the priest's antiguerrilla activities expressed deep concern at what might happen if his army was broken up.

Father Hoa has made two trips to Saigon to try to clarify the Government's intentions. He said in an interview that he planned to return to Hai Yen

Father Augustin Nguyen Lac Hoa holds no formal military title or position at Hai Yen. But in the absence of a regular army commander, he has been military leader as well as parish priest. His hope now is that, even though an official commander is to be on the spot, his unusual counter-guerrilla tactics and the strong loyalties he has established will not be lost.

The influence of Father Hoa extends beyond his small sector. Hai Yen, 15 miles square, has 1,200 men under arms to defend a population of 18,000. Most of the troops are Chinese of the Nung tribe of North Vietnam, but two companies are completely Vietnamese. American military sources fear Hai Yen would fall to the Viet Cong in six months if Father Hoa left.

Left China in 1951

The husky 56-year-old priest has become a symbol to Roman Catholics in Vietnam and abroad. He fled Communist China with several hundred followers in 1951, establishing a home first in North Vietnam, then in Cambodia and finally in 1959 in South Vietnam.

Poorly armed and led only by the priest, who had commanded a battalion in the Chinese army, the immigrants cleared the Viet Cong from the sector and gradually won the support of Vietnamese villagers.

With increasing publicity, the priest became a controversial figure. There were many who questioned his military skill—he follows few traditional practices in fighting the guerrillas. He also was supported and admired by Ngo Dinh Diệm when he was President, which made him suspect by the forces that opposed the Diệm regime.

With the downfall and death of President Diệm last November, the priest's position became shaky outside Hai Yen although the people of the sector remained almost fanatically loyal.

Unclear on Motives

Father Hoá is unclear about the reason for and the intent of the new Government directive. It conflicts with the policy of Premier Nguyen Khank [sic: actually Khánh, Nguyễn Khánh from February 2 to August 29, 1964 prime minister of the Republic of Vietnam, A/N] of seeking anti-Communist support from all organized groups across the country.

Father Hoá saw Premier Khánh two weeks ago and was reported to have received full assurances of support. Then came the appointment of an army major as battalion commander, which Father Hoá had favored, but with it a second appointment—the naming of another major as sector commander, the post the priest had held in practice.

Some Americans believe the order originated well below Premier Khánh, perhaps with army commanders who have been hostile.

CHAPTER 7

• • • • • • • • • • • • • • • • • •

Father Bosco

• • • • • • • • • • • • • • • • • •

Among the Fighting Fathers, priests, monks, or friars, the most well known (and at the same time the most mysterious) was a certain Father Bosco, who worked in the camp at Phước Thiến, in the hinterland west of Phan Rang (at the time the capital of the province of Ninh Thuận, in the central coastal area of South Vietnam); the "personal army" of his parishioners was armed by the CIA beginning in December 1961, by CIA agent Jack Benefiel, who was one of the previously mentioned Col. Gilbert Layton's men and from March 1960 to January 1964 was chief of the MOS (Military Operations Section of the CIA). The militiamen of that area were defined by the Americans as "Strikers" (in recognition of their offensive character) and answered to Father Bosco, defined by the Americans as a "Catholic monk," a most mysterious and at the same time most interesting figure.

Father Bosco (Brother Bosco or Bro' Bosco as he was called by the Americans) was cited here and there as a "missionary" or as a "monk," whose name at first glance could be presumed (erroneously) to be Italian. In reality, Saint John Bosco is a saint who is very popular among the Catholic minorities in Southeast Asia, which is why many locals named their sons Bosco, or many had the nickname Bosco, without them indicating that they were Italian, but in fact the opposite, in this case certifying their local affiliation.

In Vietnam and throughout Southeast Asia, there were many Italian and French missionaries, none of whom, as far as anyone knows, were in the ranks of the Fighting Fathers. Father Bosco was in fact 100 percent Vietnamese.

His American and South Vietnamese contacts were based at Phan Rang,[*] capital of Ninh Thuận Province, but the intense operational activity carried out by Father Bosco was in villages farther into the interior, mainly at Phước Thiến. Father Bosco was very protective with regard to his militia squads and always sought to obtain the best equipment possible. Even there, however, CIA activity was hampered by envy on the part of South Vietnamese authorities, and care had to be taken not to give these militia units better equipment than the Saigon regular army's. In addition, the American activity had to appear, at least on the surface, very low profile and "in the background." The South Vietnamese province chief always had to be involved, formally with a leading role. Otherwise, the American operators would have been turned away.[1] In Father Bosco's area as well, in addition to the CIA, the Green Berets initially operated in support, as advisors. One of these A-teams, from the 1st Special Forces Group, was detached between 1962 and 1963 at the Phước Thiến camp, rotating on a six-month basis.

Jack Benefiel's South Vietnamese counterpart, on the operational level, for his activities with Father Bosco was Trần Văn Minh, an air force officer called "Minh the Black." Trần Văn Minh was born on July 21, 1932, in Bạc Liêu, which was then in French Indochina. In 1960, he had attended the Air Command and Staff School at Maxwell Air Force Base, Alabama, with the rank of major. Upon his return to Vietnam that same year, he was appointed vice commandant of the Nha Trang air base (the area was near that of Jack Benefiel and Father Bosco), then of the Biên Hòa airfield, and, finally, vice commandant in charge of command and support of the base at Da Nang. After the coup and assassination of Diệm, on November 2, 1963, he was promoted to lieutenant colonel and director of the air force control center. In March 1964, he took command of the 62nd Tactical Air Command at Pleiku (in the central highlands), later to be transferred in September to head the 74th Tactical Air Command in the Mekong delta region. On June 19, 1965, he was promoted to colonel and nominated to be vice chief of the air force. On November 1, 1967, he was promoted to brigadier general and commandant of the air force, succeeding Nguyễn Cao Kỳ, who had left active service to pursue a political career. He was promoted to major general on June 19, 1968, and lieutenant general on November 1 that same year. On the eve of the fall of Saigon, at 0800 hours on April 29, 1975, Minh and thirty men of his staff presented themselves to the office of the American military attaché, requesting evacuation. Minh became a refugee in the United States, settling in Los Gatos, California, where he died on August 27, 1997, at the age of sixty-five.

Father Bosco's activities in the years after 1964, and his fate, remain a mystery. The CIA agent who replaced Jack Benefiel after his four-year service tour in the area has been dead for some time, and with him has

---

* Phan Rang district was, and to some extent still is, home of a large Cham minority, mostly of Muslim or Hindu religion. Phan Rang district has become a center for the maintenance of Cham culture. Much of the district is occupied by Cham people, where they have rice paddies, grape and peach orchards, goat flocks, and Brahman cattle. The towers are memorials to their kings and queens. There are several Cham sites with dilapidated towers along the central coast of Vietnam and major sites in Mỹ Sơn and Nha Trang. In the 1960s, various movements emerged calling for the creation of a separate Cham state in Vietnam. The Liberation Front of Champa (FLC, Le Front pour la Libération de Cham) and the Front de Libération des Hauts plateaux dominated. The latter group sought greater alliance with other hill tribe minorities. Initially known as "Front des Petits Peuples" from 1946 to 1960, the group later took the designation "Front de Libération des Hauts plateaux" and joined, with the all-encompassing FLC, the "Front unifié pour la Libération des Races opprimées" (FULRO) at some point in the 1960s. Since the late 1970s, there has been no serious Cham secessionist movement or political activity in Vietnam or Cambodia.

been lost the only witness who could have provided firsthand information on the later fortunes and fate of Father Bosco. Having said that, the opinion of those who lived in South Vietnam at the time is that a personality who was so exposed in the fight against communism would certainly have been killed, possibly even before the fall of South Vietnam.

In conclusion, however one might want to judge these priests, it can be said that the so-called popular forces, such as those examined in this book, were potentially the most suitable instrument to deal with the Communist guerrillas in that theater, in the villages of rural Vietnam. Following the decline and suspension of those programs, the American higher commands (and even more so the South Vietnamese headquarters) reconsidered the question only much later, seeking to remedy when it was already too late.

During the Vietnam War, a sizable number of Chams migrated to Peninsular Malaysia, where they were granted sanctuary by the Malaysian government out of sympathy for fellow Muslims.

The Cham community suffered a major blow during the Democratic Kampuchea. The Khmer Rouge targeted ethnic minorities such as Chinese, Thai, Lao, Vietnamese, and Cham people, though the Cham suffered the largest death toll in proportion to their population. Around 80,000 to 100,000 Cham out of a total Cham population of 250,000 people in 1975 died in the genocide.

ENDNOTES

Chapter 1

1. Main sources and reference on Hòa Hao, Cao Đài, and other sects in Vietnam: Jack David Eller, *Introducing Anthropology of Religion: Culture to the Ultima*te (New York: Routledge, 2007); David G. Marr, *Vietnam: State, War, and Revolution (1945–1946)* (Berkeley: University of California Press, 2013); Jefferson P. Marquis, "The Other Warriors: American Social Science and Nation Building in Vietnam," *Diplomatic History* 24, no. 1 (January 2000): 79–105; Hue-Tam Ho Tai, *Millenarianism and Peasant Politics in Vietnam* (Cambridge, MA: Harvard University Press, 1983); Jayne S. Werner, "Vietnamese Religious Society," in *The Oxford Handbook of Global Religions*, ed. Mark Juergensmeyer (New York: Oxford University Press, 2006), chapter 11, p. 109 onward; and Jayne S. Werner, *Peasant Politics and Religious Sectarianism: Peasant and Priest in the Cao Dai in Viet Nam* (New Haven, CT: Southeast Asia Studies, Yale University, 1981).

2. This according to Joseph Buttinger, *Vietnam: A Dragon Embattled* (New York: Praeger, 1967). According to Vietnamese police documents instead, Huỳnh Phú Sổ was arrested and executed on December 22, 1947, by the Việt Minh in Long Xuyen. Source: *Từ điển nghiệp vụ phổ thông* (Hà Nội: Viện nghiên cứu Khoa học Công an, Bộ Nội vụ, 1977), 574 ["General professional dictionary" (Hanoi: Public Security Science Research Institute, Ministry of Home Affairs, 1977), 574, in Vietnamese].

3. Sources on Ba Cut's trial and execution details: Buttinger, *Vietnam: A Dragon Embattled*; Jessica Chapman, *Cauldron of Resistance: Ngo Dinh Diem, the United States, and 1950s Southern Vietnam* (Ithaca, NY: Cornell University Press, 2013); Mark Moyar, *Triumph Forsaken: The Vietnam War, 1954–1965* (New York: Cambridge University Press, 2006); and David Lan Pham, *Two Hamlets in Nam Bo: Memoirs of Life in Vietnam through Japanese Occupation, the French and American Wars, and Communist Rule, 1940–1986* (Jefferson, NC: McFarland, 2000).

4. Main sources on Caodaism: Janet Alison Hoskins, *What Are Vietnam's Indigenous Religions?*, PDF report (Kyoto: Center for Southeast Asian Studies, Kyoto University, 2012), 4–6 (archived from the original on March 3, 2016); Janet Alison Hoskins, "God's Chosen People," in *Race, Religion, and Anti-colonial Struggle in French Indochina* (Singapore: Asia Research Institute of the National University of Singapore, 2012) (archived from the original on May 10, 2022, https://web.archive.org/web/20220510093220/https://www.academia.edu/1933794); Janet Alison Hoskins, "Caodaism," *World Religion and Spirituality*, 0037768610375520 (archived from the original on April 29, 2018; retrieved on August 10, 2017); Pháp Chánh Truyền ("the Religious Constitution of Cao Đài Religion"), Tân Luật ("The Canonical Codes"), and Con Đường Thiêng Liêng Hằng Sống ("Divine Path to Eternal Life"), https://web.archive.org/web/20150812211020/http://daotam.info/booksv/PhapChanhTruyen/PhapChanhTruyen.htm, consulted July 19, 2023; His Holiness Hộ-Pháp Phạm Công Tắc, *Divine Path to Eternal Life: Con Đường Thiêng Liêng Hằng Sống*, trans. Christopher Hartney and Cong-Tam Dao, https://web.archive.org/web/20150812165146/http://daotam.info/booksv/dptel/dptel.htm, consulted on July 19, 2023; and Hộ-Pháp Phạm Công Tắc. *Divine Path to Eternal Life* (Sydney, Australia: Sydney Centre for Studies in Caodaism (archived from the original on August 12, 2015). The content is similar to the source quoted immediately above, https://web.archive.org/web/20150812211020/http://daotam.info/booksv/PhapChanhTruyen/PhapChanhTruyen.htm, consulted on July 19, 2023, https://www.latimes.com/archives/la-xpm-2006-jan-07-me-beliefs7-story.html. Secondary source: Patricia Ward Biederman, "Cao Dai Fuses Great Faiths of the World," *Los Angeles Times*, January 7, 2006, consulted on July 19, 2023.

5. Estimates vary; Vietnamese government figures estimate 4.4 million Caodaists affiliated to the Cao Đài Tây Ninh Holy See, with numbers rising to six million if other branches are added. However, the United Nations found about 2.5 million Cao Đài followers in Vietnam as of January 2015. A source is Hoskins, *God's Chosen People: Race, Religion, and Anti-colonial Struggle in French Indochina*, which speaks of 3.2 million for the Tây Ninh branch alone.

Chapter 2

1. Another source, *Avvenire*, the daily newspaper of the Episcopal Conference of Italy, in its January 24, 2010, issue, speaks of almost eight million baptized in Vietnam.

2. Antôn Nguyễn Ngọc Sơn, "Giáo trình lớp Hội nhập Văn hoá Văn hoá Công Giáo Việt Nam" (2020); and http://vietcatholicnews.net/News/Html/254004.htm.

3. Anh Q. Tran, "The Historiography of the Jesuits in Vietnam: 1615–1773 and 1957–2007," *Brill*, October 2018, retrieved June 25, 2023.

4. Main source on these figures: Rev. John Trần Công Nghị, "Catholic Church in Vietnam with 470 years of Evangelization," Religious Education Congress in Anaheim, 2004.

5. Mark W. McLeod, "Nationalism and Religion in Vietnam: Phan Boi Chau and the Catholic Question," *International History Review* 14, no. 4 (1992): 31–32.

Chapter 4

1. Wesley R. Fishel, at the time professor of political science at Michigan State University. From 1956 to 1958 chief advisor of the University Vietnam Advisory Group. Fishel was an active proponent of America's influence in Vietnam, and a close friend of Ngo Dinh Diem.

2. Piero Gheddo, *Cattolici e Buddisti nel Vietnam: Il ruolo delle comunità religiose nella costruzione della pace* (Florence: Vallecchi, 1968); Thomas L. Ahern, *CIA and the House of NGO: Covert Action in South Vietnam, 1954–1963* (Washington, DC: Center for the Study of Intelligence, Central Intelligence Agency, 2000); William E. Colby with Peter Forbath, *Honorable Men: My Life in the CIA* (New York: Simon & Schuster, 1978); and David Halberstam and Daniel J. Singal, *The Making of a Quagmire: America and Vietnam during the Kennedy Era* (Lanham, MD: Rowman & Littlefield, 2008).

3. William Henderson and Wesley R. Fishel, "The Foreign Policy of Ngo Dinh Diem," *Vietnam Perspectives* 2, no. 1 (August 1966): 3–30; this quote is on page 4.

4. Main source on the coup: Ahern, *CIA and the House of Ngo*. For the final stage: the chapter "The Demise of the House of Ngo," p. 211 onward on the original printed version. Sources reported by Ahern in *CIA and the House of Ngo*, Coup Chronology (i.e., the series of cables registered as no. 2131 to no. 2152). For the report on the situation, "History of the Vietnamese Generals' Coup of November 1–2, 1963," CSHP (Clandestine Service Historical Paper) 9, Saigon Station Log and Analysis, October–November 1963, p. 9 (Saigon CIA officials put together the relevant papers); an unsigned memorial to William Colby titled "Circumstances of the Deaths of Diem and Nhu"; a memorandum for the record "Description of the Death of President Diem and Ngo Dinh Nhu," also anonymous, dated November 18, 1963; another anonymous memorandum for the record, "Colonel Anh Ba and Major General Mai Huu Xuan," dated July 28, 1975; Gen. Tran Van Don, *Our Endless War: Inside Vietnam* (San Rafael, CA: Presidio, 1978), 112; and an interview with Lucien Conein from February 19, 1992.

Chapter 5

1. It has to be considered that in some cases, the American sources on these make some confusion: the same SF Camp indicated as located in "Phan Rang (Phuoc Thien)," so referring to this specific camp, and given as established in May 1962 and closed in July 1963, indicate the relevant province as Binh Thuan, while both Phan Rang and Phước Thiến are in Ninh Thuận Province.

2. Main source on these statistics: Gheddo, *Cattolici e Buddisti nel Vietnam*.

3. Thomas L. Ahern, *CIA and Rural Pacification in South Vietnam* (Washington, DC: Center for the Study of Intelligence, Central Intelligence Agency, 2001), 74 on original printed version.

4. From CIA FOIA Covert Annex Status Report of Task Force Vietnam (May 16–28, 1962), declassified ("Approved for Release") in March 2001:

I. South Vietnam
A. Counterinsurgency Program
1. Citizens Irregular Defense Groups (CIDGs)
At point "d": The layout and construction of a training camp in Brother Bosco's village in Phước Thiến in the Phan Rang area was begun May 23, 1962. The training cadre, one half of one US Special Forces team, set up temporary quarters there on May 24, 1962.

Chapter 6

1. CIA-FOIA sources: The "Fighting Fathers" are documented in East Asia Division Job 91-00270R, box 1. The background of the Combat Intelligence Team is contained in East Asia Division Job 72-00233R, box 5; Bernard Yoh, "The Past, Present, and Future of the Sea Swallows," n.d., attachment to FVSA 14069, August 17, 1962; and SAIG 6618, December 22, 1961, the last two in East Asia Division Job 91-00270R, box 1, folder 16.

Chapter 7

1. All details in this paragraph come from the direct testimony of Jack Benefiel to the author.

BIBLIOGRAPHY

Ahern, Thomas L. *CIA and Rural Pacification in South Vietnam*. Washington, DC: Center for the Study of Intelligence, Central Intelligence Agency, 2001.

Colby, William E., with Peter Forbath. *Honorable Men: My Life in the CIA*. New York: Simon & Schuster, 1978.

Dagenais, Henry F. *The Sea Swallows: Campaigning in the South Vietnam Delta with Chinese Catholic Exiles*. Privately printed by the author, February 9, 2014.

Gheddo, Piero. *Cattolici e Buddisti nel Vietnam: Il ruolo delle comunità religiose nella costruzione della pace*. Florence: Vallecchi, 1968.

Giorgi, Alessandro. *Cronaca della Guerra del Vietnam, 1961–1975*. Vicchio, Florence, Italy: Luca Poggiali Editore, 2016.

Giorgi, Alessandro. "I Padri Combattenti." *Storia & Battaglie*, June and July 2018.

Giorgi, Alessandro. "Padre Bosco—un prete combattente." *Storia & Battaglie*, January 2019.

Harris, John Paul. *Going Local: The Buon Enao Experiment and American Counterinsurgency in Vietnam*. Sandhurst Occasional Papers 13 (2013).

McHale, Shawn F. *The First Vietnam War: Violence, Sovereignty, and the Fracture of the South, 1945–1956*. Cambridge, UK: Cambridge University Press, 2021.

Ramon Magsaysay Award Foundation (RMAF) biography of Father Augustine Hóa, Manila, 2018.

Taiwan Today Review, March 1, 1965.

Valentine, Douglas. *The Phoenix Program*. New York: William Morrow, 1990.

Online

Email exchange with Jack Benefiel.

Email exchange with Padre Cesare Bullo.

INDEX

Acheson, Dean G., secretary of state, 31

Alexandre de Rhodes, French (Avignonese) Jesuit missionary, 15

American base at Solid Anchor on the Cau Lon River; 61

Anti-Communist Denunciation Campaign, 34

Antonio Barbosa, Jesuit missionary, 15

ARVN, Army of the Republic of Vietnam, 35, 36, 40, 44, 62

Association for the Restoration of Great Vietnam (Việt Nam Đại Việt Phục Hưng Hội), secret political party formed by Diệm, 30

Ba Cụt (Lê Quang Vinh, popularly known as Ba Cụt, "cut finger," because he had cut off a finger), 11, 76

Bảo Đại, emperor, 29, 30, 32, 33

Bảy Đởm, 11

Benefiel, Jack, CIA agent, area of Brother Bosco, 5, 47, 73, 74, 75, 78, 79

Bernard Yoh, CIA collaborator, former Kuomintang officer, and Father Nguyễn Lạc Hóa's friend, 50, 56, 78

Bình Hưng, village in the Ca Mau peninsula, home base of Father Hoa's Sea Swallows, 47, 48, 49, 50, 51, 52, 57, 58, 59, 60, 64, 66, 68

Bình Xuyên, organized crime syndicate militia, 34, 42

Bishop Pierre Borie, Catholic missionary (executed), 18

Branley, Brendan, Maryknoll Father, 32

Brother Bosco, Fighting Father, 4, 5, 47, 73, 74, 75, 78

Buddhism, 9, 10, 11, 12, 21, 37, 41, 42, 43

Buddhist crisis, 21, 36, 37, 38, 41, 42, 43

Buzomi, Francesco, Italian Jesuit, 15

Cần Lao Party, 33

Cao Đài (sect), 9, 12, 13, 24, 34, 49, 51, 76, 77

Castro, Fidel, see Fidel Castro

Catholic Youth, armed formation, 25, 48

Chams, Austronesian ethnicity, 74, 75

Chen I-cheng, see Father Augustine Nguyễn Lạc Hóa

Chiang Kai-shek, Marshal, head of the Kuomintang and president of the Republic of China (Taiwan), 60

Chinese Patriotic Church, or the Protestant church of the Three Independences), 56

Chuong (Chương) Chinh Quay, major, South Vietnamese commander of the Hải Yến District, 69

Chương, Lieutenant, 52

Colby, William E., CIA deputy chief of station in Saigon, then chief of station, then chief of the CIA Far East Division,

then director of the CIA, 24, 25, 48, 50, 51, 77, 78

Combat Youth, armed formation, 25, 59

Cường Để, prince, anti-colonial activist, 10, 30

Dagenais, Henry "Hank," MACV senior advisor for the Hải Yến Special Zone from September 1967 to September 1968, 60, 61

Diệm, see Ngô Đình Diệm

Điện Biên Phủ, 23, 33

Diogo de Carvalho, Portuguese Jesuit, 15

Dominico Henares, Catholic missionary (executed), 18

Donovan, William J., former director of the Office of Strategic Services, 33

Douglas, William O., Supreme Court justice, 33

Dương Văn Minh, general, coupist, 36, 44

Emperor Gia Long, see Nguyễn Ánh

Father Augustine Nguyễn Lạc Hóa, see Father Nguyễn Lạc Hóa

Father Jean-Louis Taberd, French missionary in Siam, 18

Father Joseph Marchand, French missionary (executed), 18

Father Nguyễn Lạc Hóa, Fighting Father, 5, 24, 47, 48, 49, 50, 51, 52, 55, 56, 57, 58, 59, 60, 61, 62, 63, 64, 65, 66, 67, 68, 69, 70, 71

Father Nguyễn Văn Tâm, Catholic priest and leader (field commander), 18

Father YUN, see Father Nguyen Lac Hoa

Fidel Castro, 24

Fighting Fathers, 4, 25, 47, 59, 73, 78

Fishel, Wesley R., professor of political science at Michigan State University, 32, 33, 42, 77

Francis Xavier Nguyễn Văn Thuận, Vietnamese cardinal, 22

Francisco de Pina, Portuguese Jesuit missionary, 15

François Jaccard, Catholic missionary (executed), 18

French Catholic primary school (Pellerin School) in Huế, 28

Gaspar do Amaral, Portuguese Jesuit missionary, 15

Geneva Accords of 1954, 23, 33, 42

Gioan Baotixita, see Ngô Đình Diệm

Girolamo Maiorica, Italian Jesuit missionary, 15

Hà Minh Tri, communist, attempted to assassinate Diệm, 34

Hải Yến Special Zone or Special District, 49, 50, 55, 57, 58, 59, 60, 61, 62, 64, 68, 69, 70

Hanoi's Central Committee, 35

Hồ Chí Minh, Vietnam Communist leader, 30

Hòa Hảo (sect), 9, 10, 11, 12, 34, 76

Hòa thượng Thích Quảng Đức, Buddhist monk, 39

Hukbalahap, Filipino communist guerrilla movement, 24, 65, 67

Huỳnh Phú Sổ, founder of the Hòa Hảo sect, 9, 10, 11, 76

Ignacio Delgado, Spanish Catholic missionary (executed), 18

Jarvis, Edward, British historian, 28

Jean-Baptiste Nguyễn Bá Tòng, first Vietnamese bishop, 21

Jean-Charles Cornay, French Catholic missionary (executed), 18

José Fernández, Spanish Catholic missionary (executed), 18

Joseph-Marie Cardinal Trịnh Văn Căn, Vietnamese cardinal, 21

Joseph-Marie Trịnh Như Khuê, first Vietnamese cardinal, 21

Kennedy, John F., senator (D.) of Massachusetts, then president of the United States, 31, 33, 41, 49, 60

Lansdale, Edward G., OSS, USAF, and CIA officer, 24, 49

Layton, Gilbert B., colonel, CIA officer, 25, 47, 48, 58, 59, 73

Lê Quang Tung, colonel, commander of the South Vietnamese Special Forces, 51, 52

Lê Thi Ghâm (The Panther), Trần Văn Soái's third concubine, 11

Lê Văn Duyệt, Vietnamese general, 17

Lê Văn Khôi, general Lê Văn Duyệt's son, 17, 18

Lycée Quốc học, the French lycée in Huế, 28

Magsaysay, Ramón, president of the Philippines, 65, 67

Malayan Emergency, 35

Mansfield, Michael Joseph "Mike," senator (D) of Montana, 33

Mao Tse Tung, 55, 56

Marcel Nguyễn Tân Văn, Redemptorist brother, 22

Maryknoll Junior Seminary in Lakewood Township, New Jersey, 31, 32

Maryknoll Seminary in Ossining, West Chester County, New York, 31

McLeod, Mark, historian, 17, 77

Miller, Edward, American historian, 28, 36, 39

Minh Mạng, Vietnamese emperor, 17, 18, 27

MOS (Military Operations Section of the CIA, known by its cover name Combined Studies Division of the MAAG, later MACV), 47, 58, 73

Moyar, Mark, military historian, 28
Mr. Niep or "Nip," nickname of a brother of Father Hóa's, a lieutenant in the South Vietnamese air force. He had previously acted as a CIA agent in the north, 61
National Liberation Front (NLF), see Viet Cong
Ngia, Father Nguyễn Lạc Hóa's brother, 55
Ngô Đình Cẩn, Ngô Đình Khả's son and Diệm's brother, 27
Ngô Đình Diệm, president of the Republic of Vietnam (South Vietnam), 6, 11, 21, 23, 25, 27, 28, 29, 30, 31, 32, 33, 34, 35, 36, 37, 38, 39, 40, 41, 42, 43, 44, 47, 48, 49, 50, 51, 56, 57, 61, 62, 70, 74, 77, 78
Ngô Đình Khả, Diệm's father, 27
Ngô Đình Khôi, Ngô Đình Khả's son and Diệm's brother, 27, 29, 30
Ngô Đình Luyện, Ngô Đình Khả's son and Diệm's brother, 27
Ngô Đình Nhu, Ngô Đình Diem's brother, and chief of the South Vietnamese secret police, 25, 27, 33, 40, 42, 78
Ngô Đình Thị Giao, Ngô Đình Khả's daughter and Diệm sister, 27
Ngô Đình Thị Hiệp, Ngô Đình Khả's daughter and Diệm's sister, 27
Ngô Đình Thị Hoàng, Ngô Đình Khả's daughter and Diệm's sister, 27
Ngô Đình Thục, Ngô Đình Khả's son and Diệm's brother, 21, 27, 28, 39
Nguyễn Ánh, later Emperor Gia Long, 15, 16, 17
Nguyễn Cao Kỳ, South Vietnamese Air Force commander and politician, 74
Nguyễn Chánh Thi, colonel, coupist, 35
Nguyễn Hữu Bài, Catholic head of the Council of Ministers at the Huế court, 29
Nguyen Khanh, major general, then premier, 44, 68, 70, 71
Nguyễn Phúc Cảnh, crown prince, 16
Nguyễn Phúc Đảm, son of Gia Long's second wife, 16
Nguyễn Văn Nhung, captain, 44
Nguyễn Văn Thuận, Vietnamese cardinal, 22
No. 1001 Group, or Self-Defense Corps No. 1001, 50, 57
Nuoc, Major, South Vietnamese commander, 60
O'Melia, Thomas A., Maryknoll Father, 31
Operation Mongoose (CIA plan to eliminate Fidel Castro), 24
Operation Passage to Freedom, 24
Operation Sunrise, first phase of a South Vietnamese counter-offensive against the Viet Cong, 35

Pakhoi seminary (now known as Beihai), 55, 62, 63
Papal college (Collège General, also Pontifical College) at Pulau Tikus on the Penang peninsula in Malaysia, 55, 63
Paul-Joseph Cardinal Phạm Đình Tụng, Vietnamese cardinal, 21
Pero Marques, Portuguese Jesuit, 15
Phạm Thị Thân, Ngô Đình Khả's second wife, 27
Phan Bội Châu, Vietnamese anti-colonial activist, 29
Phan Châu Trinh, Vietnamese politician, revolutionary and patriot, 27
Phat, Father Nguyễn Lạc Hóa's brother, 55
Phoenix Program, 48
Phước Thiện, village home base of Brother Bosco's "Strikers," and Special Forces camp, west of Phan Rang, 47, 73, 74, 78
Pierre Martin Ngô Đình Thục, archbishop of Huế and Diệm's elder brother, 21, 27, 28, 39
Pigneau de Behaine, French missionary priest and Bishop of Adraa, 15, 16
Ping Hsing (see Bình Hưng, Ping Hsing was the Chinese name of Bình Hưng) political re-education centers, also "reeducation camps" (re-education camps where Diệm sent suspected Communists), 34, 41
Pontifical College in Penang, Malaya, see Papal college
Pope John Paul II, 22
Pope Pius XI, 21
Pope Pius XII, 32
popular forces, South Vietnamese regular militia 75
Ramon Magsaysay Award Foundation, 62
reeducation camps, see political re-education centers
regional forces, South Vietnamese regular militia, 62
Religious Policies and the Buddhist Crisis, 37
Saint Andrew's Abbey, Bruges, Belgium, 31
Saint Therese Seminary for diocesan priests at Pakhoi, 62, 63
School of Public Administration and Law in Hanoi, 28
Sea Swallows, 24, 25, 47, 48, 49, 50, 51, 52, 58, 59, 60, 61, 64, 65, 67, 69, 78
Shih-Wan-Ta-Shan ("A Hundred Thousand Great Mountains") area, on the border between Kwangtung (Guangdong) and Kwangshi (Guangxi), 55
Sihanouk, Norodom, Cambodian prince and prime minister, 56

Sino-Japanese war (1937–1945), 55
South Vietnamese Regional Forces, see regional forces, South Vietnamese regular militia
Special Forces A-Team 411, 60
Spellman, Francis Joseph, cardinal, 31, 33
Strategic Hamlet Program (Vietnamese: Ấp Chiến lược), 5, 35, 36, 48
Strikers, Brother Bosco's guerrillas, 73
Tây Sơn brothers, army and rebellion, 15, 16, 17
Thaddeus Nguyễn Văn Lý, dissident Catholic priest, 22
Thành Thái, emperor, 27
Thanh, Father Nguyễn Lạc Hóa's brother, 55
thầy Gioan Bosco Dòng Giuse [Friar John Bosco of the Order of Joseph], see Brother Bosco
Thích Trí Quang, Buddhist monk, 39
Thompson, Sir Robert G. K., British senior advisor in South Vietnam, 35
Thục, see Pierre Martin Ngô Đình Thục
Trần Trọng Kim, prime minister, 30
Tran Van Don, South Vietnamese general (Buddhist), coupist, 39, 44, 78
Trần Văn Minh, aka "Minh the Black," South Vietnamese air force officer, 74
Trần Văn Soái, who took the name of Năm Lửa (Five Fires), leader of the Hòa Hảo, 11
Trịnh Minh Thế, Cao Đài militia commander, 24
Tự Đức, emperor, 27
Tung, see Lê Quang Tung
US Navy SEALs, 61
Valentine, Douglas, American historian, 48
Vesak celebrations commemorating the birth of Gautama Buddha, 21, 39
Việt Cộng (also NLF, National Liberation Front), 11, 25, 33, 34, 35, 36, 37, 39, 47, 49, 50, 51, 55, 56, 57, 58, 59, 60, 61, 62, 64, 66, 67, 68, 69, 70
Viet Cong U Minh 2 battalion, 62
Việt Minh, 10, 11, 21, 23, 24, 30, 48, 56, 76,
Vương Văn Đông, lieutenant colonel, coupist, 35
Wong Lo-dai, former schoolmate of Hoa's who had become a notorious South China river pirate, 63
YUAN LO-HUA, Yuan Lo-wha, see Father Nguyen Lac Hoa
YUN LOC-FA, see Father Nguyen Lac Hoa